I0142345

Encompass

How long will you go here and there,
O faithless daughter?
For the LORD has created
a new thing in the earth —
A woman will encompass a man.
Jeremiah 31:22

Written by: CJP Navarro

Encompass

Written by: CJP Navarro

Faithless Daughter Ministries, LLC

Author photo by Cassy Mirich Photography.

Dedicated to my husband;
the love of my life and my forever best friend.
Thanks for always believing in me.
Love, c.

Acknowledgements

To Stacey, one of the most faithful friends I've ever known. Thank you for good conversation over the years I've been blessed to know you. Truly you are iron that sharpens.

To Peggy, an amazing Martha who is gracefully becoming more and more like Mary. This world needs both women. Thank you for loving me so well when I needed it the most.

Thank you both for reading my book in it's earliest stages and being so graceful with me. You are amazing women.

And to Brittany, a fellow writer and friend who led the way. Thank you!

And to my baby sister, Sara. I'm so thankful you had a rare boring weekend and actually wanted to read my book in its raw form. I'm so humbled that you read it! And forever grateful for your invaluable insights. You are such a gift. I love you dearly.

To my editor, Larry, Thank You for being you. My awesome brother-in-law who makes my heart smile.

Table of Contents

Chapter 1:

Beautiful Journey

There are still sweet things in the midst of hard ones. We just have to know how to look and see.

The wispy, tangled curls of my two-year-old illuminated in the sun-light. The deep dimple in his right cheek. The way his twin brother gallops across the room and tilts his head back letting out a hearty laugh.

Fifteen years ago, I would have never believed this was where my life would lead. In college I was the ultimate independent, ego driven girl who believed I was destined for greatness. I had absolutely zero desire to marry and rear children at all.

Growing up in a big family, helping with younger siblings and nephews, had left me yearning for a life unencumbered. An adventure is what I wanted. Maybe I would travel the world capturing the plights of man as a photojournalist. Maybe I would feed starving children in a forgotten village. Anything that would take me away from my big, loud family and the suffocating world I lived my day to day life in.

As a child I traveled enough to know the world was a lot bigger than my hometown and the principles that governed local society. My dad had taught my siblings and I to think big, to judge people by their character rather than their outward appearance, and that life is an adventure.

In those early years, before he died, life was an adventure. Every moment we could get away was spent traveling out west or to some exotic place. There were always big parties and plenty of kids around to play with. We spent the summers boating on the local lakes and courageously leaping off high cliffs into the cool mountain waters below. Life was a dream. My earliest memories were fun and exciting. Big Christmases and even bigger birthdays. Sledding and skiing in the winter months and getting warm by the fire in our cozy home.

After his death, life became stagnant. I went to school, played sports, made decent grades and hung around boys who were nothing like my father. Local country boys who couldn't understand my need for travel and adventure. Boys who went to church on Sunday, but cussed like sailors during the week.

By the time I hit middle school all I could think of was running away. I dreamed of running from what I felt to be a suffocating existence. The friends I tended to connect with the most came from rough backgrounds. Being around more traditional families made me uncomfortable and I always felt I needed to hide the past from them. But, there is no hiding in a small town. Everyone knew my story. Or at least, they thought they knew my story.

How many times did I need to hear the cashier at the store mention the mysterious, unsolved murder of the man who I happened to share a last name with before I went crazy?

'Maybe you're related to him,' they would conclude at the end of the gruesome story with a mischievous twinkle in their eye.

'He was my dad,' I would simply reply and walk away leaving their mouth gaping open in astonishment, and possibly embarrassment, for their idiotic jabber.

How many times did I need to argue with someone in my tiny high school that, 'No. My dad really is dead. No. He's not in witness protection.'

It was just too much to process. I went back and forth in my mind from trying to ignore it all, to absolutely hating the people around me.

I had to run. I had to go where no one knew my story. Where no one thought they knew my story. Too many times the words cut more deeply than anyone would ever see or understand. The girl on the school bus who told me her uncle said he wanted to shake the man's hand who shot my dad. We were kids, and maybe she didn't know what she was saying. But, it didn't matter. Damage was being done to my soul that only One Person could restore.

And that One Person would prove nearly impossible to find in that small town amidst my heartache and confusion.

In my small corner of the world we would trip over churches. It seemed every family had a family church where they were expected to attend three times a week. People would get squeaky clean on Sunday mornings, dust of the bible they had left in the floorboard of their truck all week, and walk into that building with their head held high. It didn't really matter what they did the night before, so long as the preacher didn't find out, as long as they came on Sunday mornings, put on a good face and vaguely said they were sorry for not being 'perfect'. That was the joke. I would see men slapping each other on the back laughing that they weren't perfect. But, I sure felt like we had to appear perfect, or else be the topic of local gossip.

As sad as it sounds that was the gospel as I knew it. The preacher's words were mostly about a place called Hell, and that we should feel sorry for all our wretched sins. As I grew older my 'sins' became worse and so that was called 'backsliding.' But, the trouble was, I wasn't sure what, or Who exactly, I was backsliding from. I believed in this man called Jesus. But I couldn't see Him through the fog of hypocrisy around me.

My mom would dress us girls up and take us to church like a good, southern lady. She was dutiful, kind and authentic from my point of view. And in those very early years I would cling to her faithfulness as an example and try to ignore the craziness around me. My dad, however, did not fit the mold and would not conform. He chose to stay away from the church building and gained the reputation as a decent business man who was lost and on his way to that place called Hell.

Daddy grew up in Key West, Florida and was a true child of the 60s. His mother was killed by a drunk driver when he was twelve and then a few years later lost his closest brother, also in a horrific drunk driving accident. My dad was in the car with his brother, and had tried to save him. After that he seemed to gravitate toward North Carolina where his biological, and ironically, alcoholic dad lived. My dad never completely stopped enjoying his drinks or his late-night tokes either, but he was understandably a nervous wreck anytime he was the passenger in a moving vehicle.

I often wish I could have spoken to him as an adult about losing his mother and brother at such a young age so tragically. Looking back, he never acted like the victim that I have wanted to turn him in to. He seemed to enjoy life and knew that each day was a gift. He was fun to be around. Fun to laugh with. He seemed to make others laugh and people genuinely seemed to enjoy his company. Those are the really good things I remember. The bad stuff is there, too. But, not in the way most people think.

Even though the locals didn't approve of his long blonde hair, my dad fell in love with the mountains of western North Carolina. When I would walk with him in the woods I was always amazed that he knew every tree name. He seemed at home in the woods. He seemed at peace. He loved to have a big fire going in the wood burning fireplace of the house him and mom had built. In the chilly evenings I can remember him reclining on a rug just staring and thinking. He was a deep thinker, a dreamer if there ever was one. I saw goodness in my dad.

One night my dutiful, faithful mom took us kids to a revival at the church where that preacher finally scared this six-year-old girl straight. An eternal lake of fire? No thank you! Sign me up to follow Jesus. He seems nice.

As we drove home I thought the whole way about how to tell my dad what had just happened. I recited the phrase the preacher had said over and over again to myself in the dark car, 'I asked Jesus to come into my heart.'

Walking the stairs to my dad's study I could tell I was holding my breath and began moving slower and slower, though something propelled me on. At the end of the large upstairs room that served as both my parents' bedroom and my dad's office, with more books than I could count, I could see him sitting at his desk with the lamp on. He was situated way back in his big chair with a book in his lap, staring at it intently and curling his long blonde hair around his fingers like he always did absent-mindedly. As I approached I stayed quiet as a mouse, not because I was afraid, but because I felt strange about what I had done that night and I wasn't sure if he would approve. When he noticed me he easily pulled me close and I climbed up on his lap like I had done a thousand times before and rested on his chest.

"I got saved tonight daddy," I whispered in his ear.

He smiled, hugged me tighter, and said, "That's great dear." And that was that. He approved. And I was happy and free as a bird again.

Until the day when I felt forever trapped. That day unwelcomely came when I was in the fourth grade.

That particular October morning had been cold and dark as I ran down our long, steep driveway to catch the bus. I heard the bus coming, but couldn't see it when I suddenly came face to face with a chicken. It startled me so much I almost fell back. My eyes couldn't make much out in the early morning light, but as I squinted I saw one of our chickens roosting on top of our red gate. It occurred to me that we never closed this red gate near the bottom of our driveway unless we were away traveling, so even in my state of early morning confusion something felt odd. In that moment the bus stopped at the end of the driveway. Quickly, I opened the gate and as the giant, sleeping bird startled and jumped down, I ran to get on the bus.

At school I never thought another thing about the mysterious case of the closed gate until the phone rang across the cafeteria during lunch hour. Somehow, I knew it was for me. I wasn't surprised when my teacher came to me and said I was leaving. She asked me if I knew why and I simply replied that I didn't. Though the look on my face seemed to frighten my friends and my teacher as they studied me. No one ever left school if they didn't know why, unless something was wrong.

Walking up the long hall-way of that tiny one-hall school, I felt my own smallness as I dragged my coat on the floor. It seemed too big and unnecessary now in the heat of the early fall afternoon. There were people standing in the large open door-way at the end and as I approached I could see it was my sister, four years my senior, crying in the arms of her teacher. Our eldest sister's best friend just stood watching them looking helpless. I never stopped my slow, methodical stride. They didn't seem to notice invisible me as I walked out of the school and down the steps toward a car I didn't recognize. The back door was open and I instinctively knew it was where I needed to go.

As I slid into the backseat of the unfamiliar car I found myself sitting next to my eldest sister. Her long, slender 5'11" frame was crumpled in the corner crying. When she noticed me sitting there she pulled me close and looked piercingly deep into my eyes. Her words ripped me to shreds.

"Crystal," she choked. "Daddy...daddy, has been shot. He's been killed."

At first, I just felt numb. Maybe my brain was trying to register the words she had said. But, within seconds I saw her face blur from the flood of tears that poured out of me. The pain crushed me like nothing I can ever explain.

***

That was 27 years ago. I'd like to tell you that the pain goes away. I'd like to tell you that you get over it. But that doesn't happen. The journey is much more than just getting over the death of a loved one. And, after all this time, I'm still learning that the journey is beautiful. Even now, as I sit here at my computer because I can't do anything else. The journey is beautiful.

Hearing my twins fuss because they don't want to take a nap. Listening to my older boys complain because they aren't allowed to play video games on Sunday, which my husband and I call the Lord's Day. Feeling the baby inside of me kick as I know his life hangs in the balance with my own. Not knowing if I'll see the tiny face looking at me. Not knowing if the complications with this pregnancy will end in life or death. The journey is still beautiful.

Chapter 2:

In the

Beginning

The night I was born it was literally a flood. Something crazy like nine inches or so. My dad had somehow remembered his camera at 2 o'clock in the morning and captured most of the delivery on film. My mother was smiling in every single picture. She once told me she got married because she desperately wanted to me a mom. So, there I was. The third girl to a dad who really wanted boys, and a mom who only wanted to be a mom.

Upon my arrival my four-year-old sister went to the bathroom while no one was looking and cut her hair nearly to the scalp. We joke that she hated me from the moment I was born and never quite got over it. Her and our eldest sister were only about two years apart and already best friends. I became the unwanted third wheel.

With older siblings, older cousins and their older friends always around, being the little person in the group afforded me ending up the brunt of all of their jokes and tricks. My only real ally was my aunt who had come to live with us the year I was born. In my earliest memories she was already a teenager on her way out to be married herself. When she was home I felt taken care of, but she couldn't always be around to protect little me.

At the age of six I had my first taste of beer. It was sitting open on a table and I just remember a huge group of older kids, most of them related to me, all begging me to try it. I did. I made a terrible face and sent them all howling with laughter as they ran away to be sure and not get caught when the adults walked back in the room.

And that was only the tip of the iceberg concerning the years of agony it was to be the little person in a big, loud family.

Our family history isn't perfect by a long shot. But, it is my history. It's part of my story and God did not make a mistake when He wrote it. Still, I often wondered as I grew up why my dad chose to live in our small town. Why my mom chose to stay after his horrific death. Why so many of my siblings are still there and why it seemed like quicksand to me for so much of my life. Even now, it's still a large part of me, which makes sense because my roots do run deep there.

I'm a direct descendent of the very first mayor on my dad's side. His daughter married a lawyer and seemed to have a good reputation, but after that things

31

went a little haywire in my family tree. My great-grandfather was apparently the town drunk and a terrible gambler who never seemed to win. When his marriage fell apart, my great-grandmother remarried a man who wouldn't allow her to bring her two boys with her. My grandfather and his brother had to go live with a great aunt who used them as farm-hands until they lied about their age and ran off to join the United States Navy.

Even though my dad wasn't born and raised in our small town I think I understand his pull to it during his adult years. In the 60s and 70s our town was still small enough to easily hide. The surrounding mountains a safe haven. Clean air, cool breezes, tall hardwoods and clear mountain lakes. A very alluring world for my dad compared to the tiny island of Key West, Florida he had known as a boy.

Eventually he and my mother were able to build a small cabin on a large piece of acreage surrounded by untouched US Forest Service land. Pure, wanted isolated privacy for a man who despised large crowds.

They purposefully built our home without electricity, tucked deep into the mountains, comfortably away from the crowds of our small downtown center. When people hear I grew up without power they stare in utter disbelief. But, it was actually a pretty nice existence looking back. It was simple. But, it was nice.

We had spring fed water for indoor plumbing. We had gas lighting, a gas stove and a gas refrigerator. Wood heat in the winter and cool mountain breezes blowing through our wide-open windows in the summer.

When the heat of those short summer months would become uncomfortable, my siblings and I happily walked the mile and a half down the dirt road to the lake. Our nearest neighbor was over a mile away in the opposite direction. That gravel road seemed to go on forever to me and there were no power lines along the way alerting anyone of our presence. The woods, the creeks, the rain that would beat down on the old tin roof lulling me to sleep after a day of being outside. It was all heavenly to a little girl with a wanderlust heart.

When my sisters had had enough of me tagging along I simply learned to enjoy being alone. With time I developed a love of reading and journaling and when I wasn't outside wandering, then I would stay in my room for hours upon hours just thinking, wondering, dreaming…

***

And now as an adult here I sit in my own study, filled with more books than my youngest children can probably count, absently listening to the clock tick as I think of my parents, knowing any minute I will hear the soft padding of tiny feet on the wood floors coming to look for me, their parent. In so many ways I still feel like the child. I am a child. And thankfully, the way my children can run to me, I can run to my heavenly Father when I remember that I haven't got it all figured out yet. When I need to have my head patted or my tears dried. As God was with me in my beginning, sordid as it may be, and as He was with me during those lonely days of wandering through the woods pondering my existence, He is here with me now as I sit continuing to allow my mind and heart to wander.

Those three words. In. The. Beginning.

"In the beginning God created…" It was the first verse I taught my oldest child when he could barely talk. I can still hear his small voice saying, "In the beginning God created the heavens and the earth. Genesis 1:1"

Later, it would be Jesus' best friend on earth who would give us more insight when he said another 'in the beginning…'

"In the beginning was the Word, and the Word was with God, and the Word was God." (John 1:1)

What? The Word was God? But wait, John doesn't stop there. He goes on to say that the Word became flesh and dwelt among us. Jesus. God wrapped in flesh. The Word of God walking among us. The disciples could see him, touch him, hear him and speak with him. In today's world I can still sit at the feet of Jesus and listen. The Word of God can sit safely on my book shelf and be pulled out and savored in any given moment.

And as I hear the pitter-patter of those two-year-old feet I can know that in the busyness of my day He has written His Word on my heart. On the hard days, when I can't sit and savor God's Word anew, I know He is the same. He is still my loving, heavenly Father gently leading, guiding, and molding me into who He has planned for me to be. Jeremiah 18 tells us that we are blessed when we trust in the LORD. And that man or woman is 'like a tree planted by water, that sends out its roots by the stream, and does not fear when heat comes, for its leaves remain green, and is not anxious in the year of drought, for it does not cease to bear fruit.'

When I cannot physically sit and drink in this Word of Life then I know He has faithfully been writing it on my heart. I can look and see, touch and taste His goodness in every moment. I believe with all my heart He has called me to this life of being a wife and mother. Yet, how do I react when I can't do what I love and what I've been called to do? When I can't do the dishes, or cook a wholesome meal, or hike in the woods with my boys. When I can't pick up my twins and they don't understand why. When I have to hire someone to do what I'm suppose to do.

I sit. I pray. I feel the closeness of God. I get to know Him a little better. In the times of drought our roots go deeper. Now, I feel the drought. I'm usually not feeling well enough to even read. But His Words are written on my heart. As I look at the barren trees outside I know the roots are down there working, looking, feeling their way toward the life-giving water and nutrients they need to survive. The forest will survive another winter of silence.

He tells us to be still. To know that He is God. Though this is a desert place, I will not fear when heat comes. My roots are deep in God's Word. In God Himself. I sit at the feet of Jesus and wait. When the doctors tell me one week to be hopeful and then the next not to be, I remember that I am not hopeful for health or life at all. Hope is a Person to me. And as I lean in to Him, I can feel the pain. Past and present. The pain is real and it beats us down. But as I am on my knees being crushed, that is where He wraps His loving arms around me. He bottles my tears and patiently waits with me.

In the beginning He created. He was with me in my beginning knitting me together in my mother's womb, knowing the pain that would come, and knowing it would draw me close to Him. I echo the thoughts of the twelve when the crowds would leave Jesus because His teaching was hard to hear and He asked if they would leave, too. They couldn't, they replied, no one has the words of life but Him.

Jesus. The God-Man. The Word that became flesh. The man who baffled the crowds and infuriated the religious sect. The man who dined with scoundrels and non-church going outcasts. The man who welcomed men like my dad and gently taught them what it was to love God and love their neighbor. Not for show, not with long-lofty prayers. But in the privacy of a heart of flesh with the God who sees, as Hagar, Abraham's concubine, rightfully called Him. A God who sees and knows. Who was in the beginning. That is the God I want to know.

Chapter 3:

Life Interrupted

God had to lead me out of the mountains of western North Carolina and into the frozen north to get me to my quiet place. The place where He truly stepped into my life. Where He turned my heart of stone to a heart of flesh.

Anchorage, Alaska was a true adventure. Exactly what my heart had yearned for much of my life. In my dreams I had been alone. In reality I was married with a baby in tow.

I met Jesse in college. And he wasn't part of the plan. He just wasn't. Obviously, he was God's plan all along. But back then I had my own plans for my life.

Growing up surrounded by strong, independent women had taught me that I didn't need anyone. Mom never remarried while she was raising her half-dozen children, and taking care of her mentally-ill mother, and her mentally-ill brother, and single-handedly running the Real Estate business she had started all those years ago with my father. It was perfectly natural for me to seek a career unattached from the nuisance I knew rearing a family would certainly bring.

But, when I met Jesse it was surprising how easily in step we were with one another. He wasn't like any of the boys from my hometown. He thought big thoughts and dreamed big dreams with me. We simply became best friends. When we weren't working or in class we were hiking and exploring the mountains around our university. We talked. We laughed. A LOT. He constantly made me laugh, and it felt really good. After graduation getting married was as seamless as breathing.

Then, as often happens when two kids get married, trouble soon cropped up. After three years of dating bliss, we immediately became pregnant after the wedding bells. Jesse wasn't ready to be a dad and I wasn't prepared for that. Our relationship became strained and cracked. We grew distant and dissatisfied. I began to lose hope.

We had accidentally landed jobs and bought a house in my hometown. The one place I didn't want to end up, which only added to my downward spiral. With a changed last name, I found strangers would actually talk more freely about the unsolved murder that happened years ago to the young, long blonde-haired drug dealer. Hate and anger took over my being. I couldn't make sense of anything. I knew logically that I needed to forgive and move on. But, what did that look like when my heart was a shattered stone?

And so, I decided to run. As I had done so many times in my life. Jesse and I had both planned on attending graduate school before we became parents, so I decided we could just as easily follow our dreams even after becoming parents. And I wanted to go as far away as I possibly could. Where no one would know me. Where no one would speak of things they didn't understand.

Alaska was the perfect choice. Jesse had been born there when his parents were in the military. He liked the idea of going back as an adult. I liked the idea of living out my dad's unfulfilled dream of moving us there when we were kids. Within a couple months of our decision we had packed up our F-150 with a few meager belongings, strapped our one-year-old in and headed north.

What an adventure it was. It did not disappoint my wanderlust soul. The sights. The people. Everything was exciting and new. Jesse and I almost forgot that we hadn't learned how to be married. Or be parents. We became busy with the busyness of new surroundings.

It was the summer of 2008 and our excitement was absolutely uncontainable. When we made it to Montana we laughed at the realization that we weren't even half-way there. We made it to mile zero, snapped happy pictures and kept on going. The Yukon Territory was especially memorable. Everyone we met at each outpost seemed to be hiding from something. I guess, in a sense, I felt right at home with them, because deep down I knew I was running and hoping to hide from something, too.

Anchorage itself was just an ordinary city. A lot like any other in the lower 48. But the difference was it felt like it was at the end of the world. As far as I could go from my reality. The surrounding wilderness helped my wanderlust heart as well. It was truly a terrifying place to be in the scheme of things. The week we moved there we heard of two separate Grizzly Bear attacks within city limits. Truly this was a new world for us. The same trails we walked and biked on right in town were teaming with wild life. It was a common occurrence to dodge behind a bush to let a Moose meander by. Around every turn I held my breath and jingled my little bells hoping to alarm any bear and let them know to please leave me alone. The running joke among the locals was when you hear the 'bear bells' that we were encouraged to carry, you were toast because it was probably a bear coming toward you who ate someone else's bells.

The adventure was simply being there. We only think we have mountains in western North Carolina. They say everything is bigger in Texas, but I'm saying everything is bigger in Alaska. The sights took our breath away and made my wanderlust heart skip.

When graduate school started it was still exciting. I loved meeting the people and learning what it was really like to be a part of the crowd of the frozen north. But, as the semester drew on things became more and more difficult. We were also attending an amazing church and meeting amazing people there, yet somehow, even in the midst of our excitement, it began to feel empty.

Our little basement apartment was warm at least and as the snow packed in I found myself reading the bible more and more. The days grew short and dropped into darkness. The cold creeped in and I started dreaming of the sun.

Jesse and I were both working full-time and going to school full-time. We started seeing our son and each other less and less. The American Dream was in our grasp. It was at the height of the recession but the economy in the north was booming, unlike the lower 48. We were in the right place at the right time to achieve everything we wanted.

But, soon I started waking up in the middle of the night with words of scripture on my mind. Words I never remembered reading. Still, they were there. Or, it would be a chapter and verse in a book I never read. I would get out of the bed and walk into the kitchen to look it up and find that the Words were leaping off the page speaking directly to me.

On top of all the scripture running through my mind constantly, it also seemed that every sermon at church hit me like a ton of bricks. The weight of the sermon would feel as though it was cutting off my oxygen. One Sunday I was especially moved when the preacher said chasing the American Dream was not biblical.

Not biblical? How had I never realized that till now?

He went on to explain that it wasn't the pursuit of happiness, but the pursuit of holiness. God was changing my heart of stone into a heart of flesh. And it was painful.

I was part of the crowd back then. The crowd that pressed in toward this man Jesus when they thought He was the Messiah who would overthrow the Roman tyranny. The crowd that pressed in to be healed and restored but had no real interest in knowing the Healer. The ten lepers who desperately cried out, only to forget and walk away from the One who had tenderly cleansed them and made them whole. I forgot for too many years to turn back to even say a 'thank you' to the Jesus who had always been with me. As I drove home late at night during my high school years I always felt His presence. But, I never really asked Him who He was or why He seemed interested in a nobody like me.

Jesus once asked His disciples who the crowds said he was. Then He wanted to know who they thought He was after spending more intimate time with Him. Their answer was very different from the masses.

It was in Alaska where Jesus really showed me Who He was. I dreamed of the light. I saw the light in my one-year-old son's eyes. But, when I fully understood Who was the Light, my surroundings were no longer as cold and dark. John tells us in chapter one verse four that, 'In Him was life, and the life was the light of men. The light shines in the darkness, and the darkness has not overcome it.' And later in verse nine he continues by saying, 'The true light, which gives light to everyone, was coming into the world. He was in the world, and the world was made through Him, yet the world did not know Him.'

For too long I was part of the world that did not fully know Him. I knew of Him my whole life. Believed in Him my whole life. As that six-year-old girl I was sincere that I didn't want to go to a place called Hell. I sincerely promised to follow Him. Yet, how can you really follow someone You don't know?

When Jesus told His disciples on the last night they were together before His death that He would be going away they wanted to know the way. 'How can we follow if we don't know the way?' they wanted to know. Jesus simply explains that He is the way. He is the door. Knowing Him, trusting Him, obeying Him. It wasn't enough to simply believe in Him. The book of James tells us that even the demons *believe*. Yes, even the demons believe in Jesus and are painfully afraid of Him. They are afraid of Him because He is not their Lord. They are living in rebellion against the one true King, and they know it.

It was in the frozen dark north where I finally began to learn what it meant to be a doer of the Word and not a hearer only. It was in the frozen north where God stepped into my life and interrupted my plans. He introduced Himself and woke me out of my slumber. For the first time I began to breathe and feel and see.

And here the real journey began. Taking that first terrifying step. That leap of faith where we read God's Word ready for action. Ready to bow before the true King of the universe. Ready to say YES to hard things. No matter what those hard things may be.

You believe that God is one; you do well.
Even the demons believe – and shudder!
James 2:19

But be doers of the word,
and not hearers only,
deceiving yourselves.

For if anyone is a hearer of the word
and not a doer,
he is like a man who looks intently
at his natural face in a mirror.

*For he looks at himself and goes away
and at once forgets what he is like.*

*But the one who looks into the perfect law,
the law of liberty, and perseveres,
being no hearer who forgets but a doer who acts,
he will be blessed in his doing.*

James 1:22-25

Chapter 4:

My Husband

When the Lord first removed the scales from my eyes during that dark, cold winter, the very first thing I saw, or the very first person He led me to see rather, was my husband. Jesse. This man that I had married. This man that I had stood in front of 200 people with a straight face and promised my life to. The implications of that had never dawned on me until God fully stepped into my thinking. And the weight of it rocked my world.

Here is where life get's tricky. Here is where our actions speak louder than our words. I can say I'm created new in Christ. But do my actions prove my devotion? Do my actions cross the line into being hypocritical? What does the current world say about us? That we are fake, right? Is there truth in their assumptions about us? Will Jesus really find faith when He returns? Am I a goat hiding among the Father's sheep? Will I be thrown out of the wedding feast for being dressed improperly?

What does God say? When the devil tempted Jesus, how did He respond? With scripture. When Jesus' friends tried to use worldly wisdom to thwart the will of God what did He say to them? We all know what He said to Peter. Ouch!

So, when my friends, or even my family, say it's too hard to do marriage God's way; what do I do?

When the world portrays biblical marriage as archaic and weak; what do I do? What do I say?

What the Lord began to show me all those years ago was just like the rest of scripture. They are the Words of Life. When the crowd turns away disappointed, confused, and possibly angry, I'm still sitting there at His feet saying, 'Where shall I go Lord?'

I'll never forget the moment God forced my attention to Jesse. Our only child at the time was sleeping soundly in our one bedroom. Jesse was watching tv on our one couch and I was sitting in the tiny kitchen bent over my bible, pouring over the pages as if my very life depended on it. Which it did, of course. I wasn't reading any book in particular, but rather skimming pages and stopping to read when something caught my fancy. Back then, I loved to read God's Word this way because I just wanted to devour it all at the same time.

As I skimmed the book of Jeremiah I came to the passage in chapter 31 about Rachel weeping for her children. I know now that it is the horrifying prophesy of King Herod killing all the male children under the age of two in Bethlehem around the time Jesus was born. He did this because the wise men had alarmed him to the fact that a new king was in town. And rather than share his throne he decided on drastic measures.

But at the time I first read this passage it made me think of my own dear mother. Lamenting the fact that one of her children was living so far from her. I couldn't help but smile as I thought of her, knowing how much she missed me, and so I kept reading the long passage…

Thus says the LORD,
"A voice is heard in Ramah,
Lamentation and bitter weeping.
Rachel is weeping for her children;
She refuses to be comforted for her children
because they are no more."

Thus says the LORD,

"Restrain your voice from weeping

And your eyes from tears;

For your work will be rewarded,"

declares the LORD,

"And they will return from the land of the enemy.

There is hope for your future,"

declares the LORD,

"And your children will return to their own territory."

Jeremiah 31:15-17

I had to smirk at the thought. It seemed in that moment God Himself was making this promise to my own mother instead of Rachel. Trying to shake off the unimaginable thought of going back to my hometown for any reason, I was intrigued enough to continue...

I have surely heard Ephraim grieving,

'You have chastised me,

and I was chastised,

Like an untrained calf;

Bring me back

that I may be restored,

For You are the LORD my God.

'For after I turned back,

I repented;

And after I was instructed,

I smote on my thigh;

I was ashamed

and also humiliated

Because I bore

the reproach of my youth.'

"Is Ephraim My dear son?

Is he a delightful child?

Indeed, as often as I have spoken against him,

I certainly still remember him;

Therefore My heart yearns for him;
I will surely have mercy on him,"
declares the LORD.
Jeremiah 31:18-20

Here I caught my breath just a little. How I felt like Ephraim. The 'reproach of my youth' followed me around and hung over me like a plague. My heart had been grieving my whole life, running, like the lost sheep that I was. Now, I was ever so lovingly being rebuked by the Father, chastised and loved. But He didn't stop there. His chastisement would hit harder. The Word continued.

"Set up for yourself road-marks,
Place for yourself guideposts;
Direct your mind to the highway,
The way by which you went.

Return, O virgin of Israel,
Return to these your cities.
Jeremiah 31:21

I only knew how to run. And God was asking me to return? How could I ever dream of doing such a thing when the world was within my grasp? The adventure I had always longed for calling to me in the never-ending wilderness of the north. How could He expect me to give up my dream?

And then, the next verse slapped me in the face. The words hurt more than anything anyone had ever said to me in the past.

"How long will you go here and there,
O faithless daughter?
For the LORD has created a new thing in the earth –
A woman will encompass a man."
Jeremiah 31:22

God Himself was calling me a *faithless daughter*.

'When will you stop running?' He wanted to know. 'Don't you know Me?' He asked. 'Don't you know Who I AM?' I could feel the words as they hit hard.

And, in that moment I knew I had not known Him. Not in the way I was meant to. Not in the way He had created me to know Him. How long had I been running from my past? How long had I been bottling up the pain for myself, instead of running to my Father's arms? In that moment He was teaching me a new thing. Though He had called me *faithless*, He had also called me His *daughter*. The one lost sheep He left the other ninety-nine to find. I was His. I was important to the heavenly Father. Even though I had spent years running away, He pursued me still. I was *His* daughter. And nothing could change that fact.

***

Once the Lord chastised me in that moment, He didn't waste anytime in propelling me forward for what He wanted to do in my heart. He was teaching me to look forward and to look at what was currently sitting right in front of me. I realized I had always been focused on what was behind. But, He gently pointed me to focus on my present. And presently, I sat staring at the one person He wanted me focused on.

My husband.

The man I was already married to. My best friend I had ignored and mistreated. My Jesse.

In one earth shattering evening God had my full attention. He was restoring my broken heart and giving my marriage a second chance.

And in that moment, I began the journey of learning what it looked like to wait upon the Lord while

He works out His perfect plan. He alone knows the plans He has for me. And He said they were good plans…

For I know the plans I have for you,
declares the LORD,
plans for welfare and not for evil,
to give you a future and a hope.

Then you will call upon Me
and come and pray to Me,
and I will hear you.

You will seek Me and find Me,
when you seek me with all your heart.

Jeremiah 29:11-13

Chapter 5:
The Mystery of
Marriage

My picture of marriage of course came directly from my parents. The nine-year-glimpse of ups and downs, mistakes and heart-ache. And the picture they had of marriage came directly from their own parents.

Daddy's mothers' first husband disappeared mysteriously in the Florida everglades during the 30s. She was pregnant with her third son at the time. She briefly married afterward, but that marriage ended almost as soon as it began. I can imagine during that time period the pressure a woman must have felt to remarry quickly.

Later, she met a US Navy man much younger than her. My grandfather. I hear he was a really sweet man, when he wasn't drinking. Unfortunately, it seems he drank a lot. It's been said that he would come home at night, open a bottle of whiskey and throw the top away.

I have one memory of this man being old and frail in our living room. In reality he was only in his 60s, but the years of alcohol abuse had caught him. There was a small bed set up for him with a brightly colored quilt in front of the side door, which led onto the front porch. I can see my mom opening bottles of pills for him as he took his daily meds. That's the only memory

I have of either one of my dad's parents, which is actually pretty amazing considering I was only two when my paternal grandfather died, and of course never met my paternal grandmother.

These two individuals, whom I never really knew, my dad's parents, ended up having two boys together. My dad was the baby boy of her five children, all sons. I don't know much about their marriage, except it didn't seem to last long. When my grandfather retired from the Navy, not long after his two boys were born, he headed back up to the mountains where his family had lived for multiple generations. She stayed in Key West, where she had always lived. They never officially divorced. After she died, when my dad was only twelve, he didn't go to live with his dad. Instead, he was passed around between his older half-brothers and their wives until he ran away at about the age of fifteen.

My mom's picture of marriage was perhaps a little better. But, not much. She was the firstborn, and much to everyone's astonishment, her birth seemed to bring on strange behavior from her mother. It wasn't until my mom was in her thirties that the medical community finally, officially diagnosed her mom with Paranoid Schizophrenia. My maternal grandfather went to an early grave never knowing what was wrong with his bride. He never divorced her for all her strange behavior, but I hear he would lose his temper and yell at her; and often was forced to send her to an asylum for short periods of time. It must have been incredibly hard for him. To not understand where her mind would go and why. I admire his faithfulness to her.

He died the year I was born. Grandma, my mother's mom, however, lived with us while I was growing up, so I knew her very well. She was just like another child in our home. I can't imagine the picture of marriage my mom saw through them, except that of hardship and faithfulness.

This generational confusion caused marriage to be a complete mystery to me. It seemed there was no one to look to as an example, until God pointed me to Himself.

Until then, marriage had seemed completely impossible. Only happy in silly romantic novels I read as a pre-teen. In the real world no one seemed really happy in marriage. It seemed like a lot of work and heart-ache and I couldn't decide the purpose.

Thankfully, our Creator knows we need guidance in this area. And it goes all the way back to the first couple.

When the world was perfect God created marriage. That's right. Marriage as God made it was part of the perfect universe. Today's world can hardly make sense of that. Marriage is seen as prison. Something to be laughed at. Scoffed at. But, God intended it for our good. And, believe it or not, it was part of his very good creation in the beginning.

After the fall is when things get hairy. But even then, God is not surprised by our tactics.

We are reminded in the new testament that 'Adam was formed first, then Eve; and Adam was not deceived, but the woman was deceived and became the transgressor (1 Timothy 2:13).'

Now, before you close this book and throw it across the room, please know that I myself am a woman! Just like any other. Independent. Wanting my own way. But, as God changed my heart, and I opened myself to His Word without reservation, the mystery of marriage became crystal clear. It's been a long walk for me. But, it's full of blessing.

Back in the garden we learn how God did not want Adam to be alone. Out of love and compassion for His child He created a woman. "Then the LORD God said, 'It is not good for man to be alone; I will make him a helper fit for him (Genesis 2:18).'"

Even when I was working in the business world this idea of order was clearly understood. At least in the businesses that were successful. Our society as a whole is ran this way. We have a president and a vice-president. On a ship there is a captain and co-captain. Even those who say they are 'partners' in business carry different roles. One person may be the face of the company and the other the behind the scenes number guy. And behind closed doors you better believe there is one more dominant partner making the final decisions. What works is when there is authority and a back-up to that authority.

Because God made women to be 'helpers' does not make us the lesser species if you will. We are not second-rate citizen's as sinful mankind has mistaken us for through the ages. The bible is so clear that we are of equal value, but made for different roles. If you have ever played on any kind of team you can understand this concept. Every player has a role. A talent that makes them invaluable to the success of the team. The trouble is within our American, individualized society we have trouble placing ourselves on a team at all. We want to stand on the top podium. We want the applause on center stage.

The thing is, it's okay to want to be recognized. The bible also talks about rewards given to those who run the race well. To those who persevere. God understands our desire to be applauded. He is our Creator and knows the depths of our thoughts and feelings. After the fall, He clearly told Eve what her life would be. How she would go from enjoying her husbands' authority, to despising it. And sadly, because of the fall, the husband is usually all too happy to hand it over, or expresses himself through anger when his authority is challenged.

73

The great mystery of marriage comes out fully in the book of Ephesians. It has taken me years to unpack these truths and allow them to penetrate into my core being. But, the longer I have digested this mystery, the more amazed I am at our Awesome Creator and His unyielding love for us.

The end of chapter five unpacks some hearty meat for those of us who are married. In verse 31 Paul quotes Genesis 2:24 by saying, "Therefore a man shall leave his father and mother and hold fast to his wife, and the two shall become one flesh."

How many marriages have I seen fall by the wayside because of a direct violation of this simple, yet profound command? It's staggering. And the jokes I hear about how God didn't command the woman to leave her parents, just the man, are the worst. A simple Language Arts class could easily debunk that ridiculous myth.

Becoming 'one flesh' is more than our current sex driven world will allow us to first understand. When God says two people shall be one flesh, He means they will literally become *one person*. A woman can not be one with her husband when she calls home every other day. The old saying, 'my other half' is a valid one and desperately needs to make an appearance in American Christianity.

I've watched women over the years who look to their parents, friends, co-workers, or whomever to be their confidant and advisor, when if their first phone call would simply be to the man they promised to become one with, their heart-aches and pains would more than likely grow less frequent. When a woman puts her husband above everyone else in her life he can feel it. It fuels him to be a better man.

Proverbs 31 gives us insight into this great mystery. Verse 16 starts out by saying, '[a]n excellent wife who can find?' Indeed! It is not natural to us in our fallen state. We can only become excellent husbands and wives through the power of God's Holy Spirit changing our hearts.

As the chapter goes on to describe the attributes of an excellent wife I especially love the parts that mention how her behavior affects her husband for good. Verse 23 says, "[h]er husband is known in the gates when he sits among the elders of the land." In our world, that would translate that he has a good reputation and is thought well of. Notice this comes as a direct result of his wife's excellence!

At the end of the chapter God paints a clear picture of the reward of her labor. The reward of being a good helper to her husband is this:

Her children rise up and call her blessed;
her husband also, and he praises her:

"Many women have done excellently,
but you surpass them all."

Charm is deceitful, and beauty is vain,
but a woman who fears the LORD
is to be praised.

Give her of the fruit of her hands,

and let her works

praise her in the gates.

Proverbs 31:28-31

I've attended many bible studies where us ladies just wanted to sit around and scoff at this chapter in the bible. We had every excuse in the world. But, over the years the Lord has gently taught me that it is possible to be praised by my husband through the power of the Holy Spirit. When we simply take God at His Word, our world can begin to change.

Chapter 6:

Laughter is

Medicine

After that fateful night, when the Lord graciously turned my attention to my husband, I started seeing my whole world in new light. The Word of God spoke to me in ways it never had before. The Word became alive to me.

In the darkness of that cold, dark Alaskan winter there was a Light illuminating and warming my heart. My heart of stone was becoming a heart of flesh.

Yet, even this new oneness with my heavenly Father did not automatically heal my broken marriage, nor anything else that was broken in my life. It was a gradual shift. A shift from selfishness, to selflessness. Moments of intimate worship and allowing a friendship with this man Jesus to form.

He opened my eyes to see Jesse for what felt like the first time. Up until this point I had always assumed responsibility as the 'spiritual leader' in our relationship. I was the one who grew up in church, not Jesse. I was the one who knew all the children's bible stories, not Jesse. I was the one with all the 'knowledge,' not Jesse.

But, when I stopped leading and started looking. Started actually seeing him for the first time, I was shocked. He came to believe in Jesus in his early twenties. He didn't know all the children's bible stories, but he seemed to know Who Jesus was and felt very comfortable with Him. I noticed his quiet, gentle spirit next to my sharp, demanding one. I noticed his playfulness with our son. And his willingness to work hard for his family without any complaint.

Without knowing it before, my husband was emulating Christ in his every day life. He was growing in his own relationship with the Lord, when I wrongly thought he had a lot of catching up to do with me.

The shift came when I began to look up to Jesse. I took my hands off the reigns and watched him quietly pick them up. He was leading us into deeper communion than I ever could. It was slow and thoughtful, where I operated fast and without reservation. Patience was being poured into my soul. Sometimes I choked on it. But, when I dug into God's Word I knew it was right and that I wasn't only trusting my husband, it was about trusting my Savior.

The road I had to take to get to the place of laughter with my husband was bumpy at best. When God showed me how I had neglected Jesse to get my own way the air was taken out of my lungs. I hadn't meant to disregard my marriage. I simply didn't know what biblical marriage looked like. But, ignorance is never a good excuse in any case. And this was no different. If I was honest with myself I knew deep down there had to be a better way.

On our two-year-anniversary we went out on the first date I can remember taking as a married couple. I don't remember what restaurant in Anchorage that we ate at. But I do remember feeling awkward. Sitting in that booth with the low lighting and romantic dinner for two seemed so foreign to me I wanted to run away. I was so disconnected to the man sitting across from me boring into me with those deep, dark brown eyes. I didn't know him anymore. We didn't know each other. God had been changing us both, and I hadn't fully noticed until I had to sit face to face with Jesse, alone.

Thankfully, our Heavenly Father was watching out for us and had a few tricks up His sleeve. After that awkward dinner we decided to go see a movie. We had been working and going to school so much that we had no idea what was playing. As we walked up to the cinema we stared blankly at all the posters, wondering what to pick. Everything had a rated R symbol, and we hadn't read any of the reviews to know why they were rated R, so they didn't appeal to us. Finally, one poster caught our eye. It was literally the only movie playing that night without a rated R on it. The name of the movie was Fireproof.

At first, we thought the movie was a little silly. Obviously low budget. But by the end, we were speechless and we walked out of the theatre that night holding hands.

Though this wasn't the night we laughed together, it was the night we began to enjoy each other's company again.

After that night, life took a dramatic turn for us.

Everything happened so fast it's hard to explain. Even now, looking back, I just remember a whirlwind. One night, Jesse said he felt like the babysitter knew our son better than we did. I had read that scripture in

Jeremiah and also felt like we were headed in the wrong direction. It's like when you realize you've veered completely off-course and are hundreds of miles from where you are supposed to be. It feels incredibly frustrating, but there is nothing left to do but turn around and return the way you came. Otherwise, you will never reach your rightful destination.

I just remember sitting in that tiny kitchen of our cozy basement apartment staring blankly at one another. The moment was terrifying. But peaceful. There were no words as we knew what we had to do. God had changed us and He wanted us to return home.

A few short months later we found ourselves back in North Carolina living in another basement apartment. This time on the charity of some friends.

Jesse found himself working five part-time jobs to support his growing family. And I felt helpless as no one would hire a woman with a growing belly and a toddler in tow. We were back in a terrible economy and circumstances literally forced me to become a stay-at-home mom. The one thing that was never on my radar.

Our circumstances looked bleak. But our hearts were full of peace. It was unexplainable. It really was the peace that surpasses all understanding at work in our lives daily. We were living out Philippians 4:6…"do not be anxious about anything, but in everything by prayer and supplication with thanksgiving let your requests be made known to God. And the peace of God, which surpasses all understanding will guard your hearts and your minds in Christ Jesus."

That scripture is still Jesse's favorite to this day. During those days of hardship God taught us some valuable lesson's we can never forget. Though Jesse was gone from home before I woke up and came home after I was in the bed at night, there was a sense of joy in our lives that we couldn't explain. Joy that was missing when we cared more about chasing the stars, than actually knowing the One who made those stars. Up above Philippians 4:6 Paul tells us to 'Rejoice in the Lord always.' Then he repeats himself by saying, 'again I will say, rejoice[!]'

Where does this joy come from? It was quite clear it did not come from circumstances. We were stripped bare by worldly standards. Jesse went from working on his Master's in Business Administration and managing the most elite health club in Anchorage, to delivering pizza's in tiny town, USA. I went from almost obtaining my desired graduate degree and landing my dream job, to being an invisible full-time mom. The one thing I never thought I would do. Our pride was crushed in one fell swoop.

We went from making good money to selling most of our possessions, liquidating our assets, and draining our savings and investments. We were able to hold on to our small cabin in the woods and one vehicle by the grace of God. He clearly wanted us living at that moment in time in the small town I had grown up in and had tried so hard to run away from. Though we were able to keep paying for our tiny home, the market crash had rendered it completely upside down. It would be years and years before the market would catch up to what we owed the bank. We were stuck.

Yet, for the first time in my life I didn't feel suffocated or have the need to cut and run. I had only joy in my heart and one purpose on my mind. Jesse. I wanted to be the wife God was calling me to be.

I devoured books on biblical marriage during those months of first being at home without a car. Some of them were rubbish and fluff, but the meatier ones stopped me in my tracks. They were the ones that didn't apologize or make excuses for scripture. It was there. Staring at me in black and white. No more excuses. No more looking at the world for relationship advice. No more looking at our modern churches and listening to the bickering about outdated, archaic scripture. When I read it for myself I saw marriage as God intended. And it was still good. Even after the fall, it was still good.

As I read and studied all I could I began to put what I learned into practice. The results were astounding. Jesse responded.

As I joyfully served him. Loved him. Respected him. He began to look at me differently. He held his head a little higher. He worked a little harder. He laughed. With me.

I'll never forget it as long as I live. When there is no laughter in a home, I'm not entirely convinced we know what is missing. Until it returns.

We were lying in bed late one night. I said something funny and Jesse let out a hearty, belly-splitting laugh. It alarmed me so much that I caught up my breath, eyes-wide, frozen in the dark. He didn't seem to notice and just kept on laughing. It must have felt good, because I realized I couldn't remember the last time I had heard him laugh like that. Like you would do with your best friend. In that moment I savored the fruit God was giving me. My husbands laugh had returned to our marriage and it was sweeter than anything I had ever known.

Through the years since that night I have come to learn just how necessary laughter really is. When daddy was still alive we laughed all the time. Laughter permeated our very existence. But, afterward it seemed I was surrounded by Christians who didn't believe in laughter. It seemed that to be a good Christian meant to be serious and forlorn. Shoulders sagging, face drooping, shaking their head in whispered talk of how hard things were. Of how difficult life is and won't Jesus just come back and take us from this wretched place, and on and on…

Is that really how scripture depicts life for a believer?

How could King David dance the way he did and be forlorn at the same time? How could the Israelites celebrate as many times a year as they did and not laugh?

No. Laughter is good. And, though I do believe laughing in itself, unlike joy, is based more on circumstance, I have learned how to laugh at the daily things in life. That is the secret I'm finding. Finding laughter. Allowing myself to lighten up enough to see that life is worth laughter.

My dad was always surrounded by laughter it seemed. Adventure seems to breed laughter. As he held me up to the rope swing too high for my little arms to reach, and told me to hold on tight, he pushed hard propelling me over the lake below as I screamed with delight.

"Now let go!" he yelled. I hit the water just right and came up laughing with my dad. I'm sure a lot of today's helicopter parents would have screamed in horror at the sight of him putting his little girl in what some would perceive as only danger, surely to be avoided at all cost.

If only they could see living in fear
is far more dangerous.

The New International Version puts it this way in Proverbs 17:22: "A cheerful heart is good medicine, but a crushed spirit dries up the bones."

The Good News Translation says it even more clearly, "Being cheerful keeps you healthy. It is a slow death to be gloomy all the time."

Yet, even with this truth in scripture I still grew up around Christians who basically modeled for me how to die a slow death. My husband read a book recently that said, 'most people die in their mid-twenties, but aren't buried until their 70s' (Les Brown, Live Your Dreams). Sadly, that seems even truer in the bible-believing community. And the very bible we claim to believe in tells us it's good for us to LAUGH!

I admit I didn't laugh very much after my father was killed. But after that fateful night when my husband suddenly burst into laughter my heart began to stir. I see now that laughter is living. I feel alive when I laugh. And the same way it is a pure delight to hear my own children laughing, our Heavenly Father is beaming as His children find reasons to laugh, too.

Now, everything makes me laugh. When my husband takes our young boys and climbs to the top of the giant waterfall near our house, I can't help but laugh at their crazy adventure, even when the neighbors are all clutching their chest's in disbelief. I laugh when my adventure-loving husband strips down to his underwear and plunges into the forbidden ponds on top of our mountain, much to our boys' delight. I laugh when one of my son's, who was only six at the time, swings high out over the jagged rocks of the rushing river to plunge into the deep water beyond, screaming with pure delight, even as most of the adults watching wouldn't dare be so bold. I laugh knowing he has so much of my dad's personality wrapped up in his own.

Dad was right when he said life was an adventure. If it's not, it should be. We weren't created to be timid beings. Do you really picture King David as a timid little boy? I don't see a timid little boy killing a bear or a lion to protect his sheep. A timid little boy didn't stand face to face with a murderous giant unafraid.

Jesus Himself was a carpenter by trade. Have you ever met a carpenter? My grandfather and my dad were carpenters. My sisters' husbands are carpenters. Their hands are not smooth and clean. They are rough and calloused. Their clothes are usually filthy, and they smell of sawdust and sweat. Their skin in bronzed and rough from long hours in the sun. No, the man Jesus was surely not soft.

I want my boys to grow up to be men like Jesus was when he walked this earth. Men like King David who boldly followed after God and led his kingdom well. Men like the apostle Paul who endured treacherous seas, torture, hunger and thirst all to spread the gospel. Men who aren't afraid to live and be bold in the Lord.

Living is synonymous with laughter. It never ceases to amaze me that when I ask my husband or our growing boys what they need for me to do, how I can serve them better, they always say the same thing: "We just want you to smile. We love to hear you laugh and see you smile."

Recently, I stood helpless as my adventurous twin boys egged one another on as they climbed the steep embankment behind our house. On and on they kept climbing until I could barely see them in the woods. I could hear their chatter, but as they started to disappear from my sight my heart clamped up. My face soured and I began to panic just a bit. When I yelled for them to come back I saw two little heads immediately pop out from behind the trees to stare down at me, their helpless mother who would compromise the health of the baby growing inside of me if I had to scale the cliffs trying to save my twin toddlers.

I had to laugh at the ridiculousness of my situation. Here I was home alone with these two adventurous boys, men in training, with no way to rescue them from themselves. Until the moment I lost complete sight of them I had kept my silence, wanting them to have their fun. But, they are not yet three-years-old and so I knew they weren't quite ready to go trapesing all over our mountain completely alone. Not yet.

Thankfully, they obediently slid down the mountain, back to the safety of their now smiling mom. I couldn't help but laugh with these two little men. They were filthy. Covered from head to toe in mud but without a scratch and beaming from ear to ear. Their eyes were dancing with delight as they looked into mine searching for how I felt about their perilous adventures in rock climbing.

As I laughed they ran to hug me. The moment was sweet because they knew I approved. Their little hearts yearn to be men who are bold enough to live. And the last thing they need is someone stealing that laughter from their eyes. Because without laughter, life is cold and stagnant. Drying up the bones. Waiting to die.

Chapter 7:

Joy comes in the

Mourning

When my marriage was finally on the mend all those years ago, God began to transform who I was in a million different ways. My thinking was radically changed by His grace and I eagerly began the transformation from independent me, to simply being Jesse's wife.

Our circumstances where changing, too. Jesse had landed a full-time job that paid the bills just in time for baby number two to be born. Though we had true contentment during the time of struggle, we now welcomed a slower pace of life that meant Jesse could actually spend evenings with his growing family and we could learn how to spend time with one another. We knew God was taking care of us and leading us into a new chapter.

Though many people would try to tell us moving back to North Carolina was a huge mistake, we would never agree. We knew God had called us back to my hometown. He was changing us and molding us into who He wanted us to be. Swallowing our pride in one giant gulp was the best thing that ever happened to us.

As time kept moving us along, I kept plugging along with my deep studies about biblical marriage and parenthood. God was stretching me in unimaginable ways during this time of my life and it mostly felt really good to know He was working on me. Molding me and making me more and more like His Son.

However, as I continued searching the scriptures and growing in my walk with getting to know Jesus, there was one glaring thorn in my side. One thing I still could not face. An old wound that would still hurt. The reason I ran away from my hometown in the first place. That one thing in my life I was still clinging to even after He had given me my heart of flesh.

That same excruciating pain from my childhood. It still haunted my dreams and crept in at the most inconvenient times unaware. The pain that would surprisingly hit me all the more as God molded me to Himself.

At first, I thought He would simply take the pain away. That He would somehow magically wave His wand in the sky and all the hurt would vanish. But, as I drew near to Him and sat at the feet of Jesus, I saw and learned what it meant to mourn. I began to see the tears on the face of the Man of Sorrows Himself.

Suddenly I could see the grief of God. While He was walking among His very own creation He was full of grief. Jesus cried real tears at the tomb of his friend, Lazarus. He openly lamented over the coming destruction of Jerusalem when He cried, "O Jerusalem, Jerusalem, the city that kills the prophets and stones those who are sent to it!" (Matthew 23:37)

My grief was no stranger to my Creator. For God is grieved in His heart, too. And, as I learned about His grief throughout the history of time, I began to understand my pain was a blessing. Satan may have meant it for evil, as he did with Job, but God knew in the end it would be used for good. Goodness does triumph in the end. I know the end of the story. And goodness triumphs.

The journey to get to that end is marked with suffering. Not because God is unjust, but because we broke His beautiful creation. He doesn't deaden the pain inside of us. Not because He is cruel, but because He loves us too much to allow us not to feel.

Deep pain can and does lead to deeper joy.

When people meet me today who don't know my past they sometimes mistakenly look at my outward circumstances to conclude why I must be smiling and cheerful. And, that hurts, too. Not being understood hurts. We all want others to understand where we are coming from. But, it is only God who will truly ever know the depth of our scars. Only He knows. And, so we must bring our pain to the One who knows.

I've been around long enough to know everyone has hurt in their life. If you live you will suffer some sort of loss. Sometimes it's the pain that sends us running that much faster into our Father's arms. Not always, but sometimes.

Some of the most joyful people I've ever met have lived lives marked with tragic circumstances. Other's I've met are the most bitter people who have lived relatively easy lives.

So, what is this joy and where does it come from?

As Christians we are actually commanded in scripture to rejoice. My favorite verse, Psalm 118:24, tells us plainly that, "This is the day that the LORD has made; let us rejoice and be glad in it."

Are we rejoicing in the LORD today? What does He mean compared with other scripture that tells us it's better to go to a house of mourning than one of feasting? This coming from the same God who instituted numerous days of feasting and celebration in the Jewish culture? On the surface it seems to contradict. But like all of scripture, on every subject, when we dig a little deeper, the mystery is made known to us.

Seek and find. Another promise of our Creator. Don't stop seeking and finding Him. He never disappoints.

I once read that joyfulness is a direct result of thankfulness. That was the beginning of understanding joy for me. Another preacher said joy is Jesus. And yes, Joy is a Person. Directly sent into us by His Spirit. Joy is most definitely a part of who He is.

But in our broken world, I have found joy is far deeper and wider than we could ever fathom, if only we could first learn how to mourn like the Father does. When we begin to mourn like Him, we can begin to see what His grief over our brokenness looks like. And then, He can begin to lead us into His uncontainable, multifaceted joy.

Jesus has taken me and shown me what deep, beautiful joy looks like.

Joy is having your heart burst on your wedding day as your dad's only son, your younger brother grown into a man, walks you down the aisle. Joy is having my cup run over when I laugh with my children and think of how much my dad enjoyed laughing with me and my siblings. Joy is when I name my firstborn after daddy and think how much he would have enjoyed seeing this beautiful baby boy. Joy is seeing my boys run and play with their amazing daddy, only to remember the brokenness of my own childhood. Joy is feeling immense pain, bone-crushing pain, yet genuinely finding reasons in every moment to smile and laugh through your tears.

You see, my whole life, I have been in the house of mourning. My whole life has been marked by the deepest of sorrows. Jesus, the Man of Sorrows, holds me close as I mourn. He knows my pain.

The pain that does not go away with time. The pain that wakes me up still and wrenches my soul when I think of my daddy being shot in cold blood. A murderer still at large, free and clear.

My dad was on crutches that morning. The crutches were in the back of his truck as he drove to work. He had a 9 o'clock meeting that never existed. A ploy set up to get him to the bottom of our driveway on time. To stop at the closed red gate and have to hobble out of the truck to grab his crutches. But he never reached for those crutches and he never opened the gate. They were waiting for him, and even after watching his nine-year-old daughter get on the school bus, their evil intent was not thwarted. They shot my dad point blank and left him dead, face down in the driveway. He had looked so handsome that morning in his soft light blue sweater, his familiar jeans and typical brown belt. My handsome daddy. Clothes ruined. Body broken beyond repair.

The pain hits me now, 27 years later, just as hard as it did the day it happened. I have lived most of my life in the house of mourning.

And yet through my deep, unquenchable mourning I have learned the meaning of joy. Joy does come from a thankful heart and it does come from Jesus Himself. But, it is made perfect through our pain only if and when we allow it to penetrate our heart of flesh. A heart of stone is only capable of anger and hatred. A heart of stone can not feel. When God turned my heart of stone into a heart of flesh I felt the pain of my dad's murder more intense than ever before. The wounds I had bound up were reopened so the true Healer could properly bind up my broken heart.

Only Jesus can bind the broken-hearted. Notice He doesn't say it will be made new in this life. But, bound. I imagine Him literally picking up the pieces, of my now heart of flesh, and holding them together as He binds them with an old blue cloth. It is a messy business, but He doesn't mind my mess. My brokenness is literally being held together by Him.

I have not left the house of mourning as I grow deeper in His joyfulness. It is hard to comprehend unless you have lived it. The celebration of a wedding day. Your heart is truly glad and swelling with joy. You love the people attending and feel truly blessed in the moment. Knowing it is a gift from God Himself. Yet, there is sadness on your heart because the one person not there will never be forgotten. His absence is always felt. On the happiest day of your life there are tears spilling into the joy. And so, Jesus patiently stands by my side and holds my hand as I walk through the pain and the joy simultaneously.

Who better to understand than Him?

The Man of Sorrows who drew crowds of thousands. The Man of Sorrows who mesmerized the masses. How could so many be drawn to a sorrowful Person? Because Jesus was Light in the midst of His sorrow. Despite His sadness over the state of His children He still smiled at them and showed them kindness and compassion. He was Light walking among the darkness. He gave thanks for His daily bread and joyfully served others. His joy was deeper than circumstances. His joy was complete in His relationship with the Father.

When other's look at me and wonder about my joy, I want to tell them it is not because my current circumstances may appear better than theirs; it is because of my relationship with the Father. I had this same joy even when I was home alone with two toddlers, with no car and no money to buy food. My relationship with the Father, not my circumstances, was and is always the source of my joy. The Father who knitted me together and knows me by name. The Father who knew the days of my dad's life on this earth before he was even born.

'…in Your book were written, every one of them, the days that were formed for me, when as yet there was none of them.' (Psalm 139:16) My dad's death may have been a surprise to me, but it was no surprise to our loving, heavenly Father.

The song "Your Love Never Fails," by the band Jesus Culture, is constantly playing in my head. Especially after a particularly rough day with the kids. When I'm worn out and weak and after finally getting them all settled for the night, instead of finally getting to relish in some alone time, in walks my husband who needs me. I always feel needed in this life of raising a bunch of boys and having to remember that I'm called to be a wife even before I'm a mom. But, Jesus was also always needed. When He would try to slip away to be alone and rest, the crowds would find Him.

I love that He never turned them away in those moments when He must have been exhausted. His strength and joy came from the Father and because of this He was able to feel compassion for the people that needed him.

When I feel crushed by the pain that creeps in when I least expect it and I'm overwhelmed by the people in my life who need me constantly, that song comes to my mind and I say those words under my breath, usually when I'm pulling myself out of bed, I sing to myself...'there may be pain in the night, but joy comes in the morning.' It reminds me of the gift of today. That we are not promised tomorrow. We only have today.

The pain of my past is a constant reminder of this. And I think my dad knew this very well. He seemed to live life to the fullest. To know what a vapor we really are. When we know that, it changes everything.

As my dad's only son, the pride of his youth, now grown into a man, stands at the alter marrying his own stunning bride, the joy God gives me in that moment takes my breath away. I am so proud and thankful for the man my younger brother has become.

But, the pain stabs at me still, as the seating confusion in the busyness of the wedding festivities causes my mom to somehow sit alone in the front row.

There is this one random, beautifully decorated empty chair beside her where our dad would have been sitting. The chair unintentionally reserved for someone of honor who was clearly missing. Not on purpose. But, it happens still.

Somehow, there is always this painful reminder of our brokenness. And the reminder of the absence of this one man, our beloved daddy, who would have been so proud of his son on his wedding day, hits me hard and I have to fight to simply breathe. I can not hold myself together in this painful and joyful moment, but thankfully Jesus is with me. Keeping my heart bound tight. Holding me together as I need to be held.

As I sit and smile, and choke on my tears, the joy and the pain come rushing out together in the beauty of that gift of a moment. God's joy, lovely and beautiful, yet always mingled with the very real pain of our brokenness.

And so, my joy comes in the mourning. *In the mourning.* And my joy is made complete only in allowing myself to feel the very real pain of this life, not pretending everything is perfect or that I've somehow reached a stage of perfection, but by feeling the pain intensely and then leaning deeper in to Jesus Himself. The only One who knows how to properly bind up my broken heart. He holds me together, as this life threatens to tear me apart. Always.

Chapter 8:

Forgiveness

As I sit and wait in the local coffee shop, I see my old friend slip in and silently scan the tables for me. She slips in to the seat across from me and I smile. A reassuring smile that she has nothing to fear in this moment of uncertainty. The words pour from her as her eyes brim timidly with repentant tears. She asks my forgiveness for old hurts. My answer surprises her as I gently say that in my heart she was already forgiven long ago.

You see, forgiveness does not need to be asked for in order to give it. Though we are commanded in scripture to run to the brother or sister we have wronged, no where does it say the one hurt is to withhold forgiveness until it is asked for.

Jesus forgave us while we were yet an enemy. While we were hating Him, throwing insults and guilt upon His innocent head, He looked to the Father and lovingly said, "Father, forgive them for they know not what they do." (Luke 23:34)

Forgiveness is birthed from Love. God is Love. And as His children we are called to live out this beautiful forgiving love on earth. Not from obligation, but from organic desire. As the apostle Paul rightfully pleaded to Philemon in asking him to forgive a former slave who had ran away, he wrote this truth, "but I preferred to do nothing without your consent in order that your goodness might not be by compulsion but of your own accord." (Philemon 14)

We don't forgive because we are afraid of God. We forgive because we *love* God. In desiring to forgive our brother or sister our fellowship with each other and our Father is that much sweeter. Paul goes on to drive this point home when he explains further to Philemon and writes, "[f]or this perhaps is why he was parted from you for a while, that you might have him back forever, no longer as a bondservant but more than a bondservant, as a beloved brother…both in the flesh and in the Lord." (Philemon 15,16)

Without forgiveness there is too much room for bitterness to grow. And that bitterness will suck the life out of you and turn your bones to ash.

Thankfully, as God restores us He can teach us to forgive one another. As Ezekiel looked out over the dead, broken bones there suddenly came the very breath of God bringing the dry bones back to life. In Him we have our being. Worshipping Him in spirit and truth means allowing Him to govern our thinking and leading us to act out his awesome love in this broken and dark world.

Years ago, when God took my own heart of stone and turned it to a heart of flesh, I realized how much hate and bitterness resided there. I knew I had to allow Him to root it out and I knew it would be uncomfortable and painful at times. It's one thing to forgive a friend who I know didn't mean to wrong me. But, forgiving a true enemy is where we ultimately take up our cross and follow Jesus into the treacherous storms. The battle is real. The enemies are great, but God is greater still.

As a young child the hate took root and grew for too long. My hate of course was primarily directed, like an arrow, toward the one man who I believed had murdered my dad. There is not proof, and I will never say he had anything to do with it beyond a shadow of doubt. But this was the man my dad had testified against. The man my dad had single-handedly put behind a cage of cold, steel bars for twenty years. The man who was released from prison nearly twenty years after my dad had been dead that same amount of time.

This man who would be sitting in the same coffee shop I walked into. This man who had many friends still in our small town. This man who should have made me shudder to think of even going near. But, perfect love casts out fear. And my God would not allow me to be afraid.

Instead of allowing me to focus on this man and what he may or may not have done, God caused me to stare into my own reflection.

"…Whoever does not love abides in death. Everyone who hates his brother is a murderer…" (1 John 14b & 15a).

I had hated this man for as long as I could remember. The hate penetrated my very being. The anger that would accompany was nearly uncontrollable at times.

And here, where I felt my hate was justified, Jesus gently took me by the hand and simply shook His head no. My sin was just as bad. My heart had been just as bare. My intent just as evil. I had murdered in my heart and mind and soul, when it was supposed to be filled with God's forgiveness and love toward someone who was made in the image of our common Creator.

Forgiveness does not make the sin right. Forgiveness does not say I am allowed to put myself in God's rightful judgment seat. Jesus sits at the right hand of the Father, judging the nations perfectly, not me. And if Jesus says they are forgiven, then they are. I don't know the heart of every man. Only Jesus does. And His voice is the final cry.

Peter asked the Lord how many times we should forgive someone and Jesus said in a nutshell that we should forgive them an unlimited amount of times. How many sins has Jesus forgiven us? Too many to count? Mine are too many to count. And He has forgiven them all. How much more am I to forgive a fellow human being who is struggling beside me in this broken world.

The parable Jesus tells of the unforgiving servant explains this concept well. After the master forgave the outlandish debt of one of his servants, the servant finds another servant on the street who owed him a very small debt. The parable ends with this:

"Then his master summoned him
[the unforgiving servant]
and said to him, 'You wicked servant!

I forgave you all that debt
because you pleaded with me.
And should not you have had mercy
on your fellow servant,
as I had mercy on you?'

And in anger his master delivered
him to the jailers,
until he should pay all his debt
[that would have taken
longer than a lifetime to pay off].

So also my heavenly Father
will do to every one of you,
if you do not forgive your brother
from your heart."

Matthew 18:32-35
*brackets mine.

Once I truly realized the implications of unforgiveness and how it choked out true communion with the Father, I melted. I truly forgave. Not from obligation, but from love. God's Love was bigger than my pain. God's Love was bigger than the hate I had felt.

As I would see him who I hated, I began to really see him. An old man with a cane. Tired. Perhaps still an enemy of God. I would speak with him. I would smile and show Love that now permeated my very being. Others ridiculed me and said I was crazy. But I wasn't crazy. I was simply in love with Jesus. The Man of Sorrows acquainted with my grief. The God-Man who forgave me as He was dying on that cross in my place. His forgiveness had stretched far and wide, even reaching far into the depths of my own broken soul.

Yes, I found I could forgive the men who shot my beloved dad in cold blood, whomever they are. If God could forgive us for murdering His innocent, perfect, beloved Son, then I could forgive also. No matter how many times it hurt. No matter how much the pain ripped me apart. Jesus is always near. He will always bind up my broken-heart.

He was despised and rejected by men;
A man of sorrows, and acquainted with grief;

And as one from whom men hide their faces
he was despised,
And we esteemed him not.

Surely, he has born our griefs
and carried our sorrows;
Yet we esteemed him stricken,
Smitten by God, and afflicted.

But he was pierced for our transgressions;
He was crushed for our iniquities;

Upon him was the chastisement
that brought us peace,

And with his wounds we are healed.
All we like sheep have gone astray;

We have turned – every one – to his own way;
And the LORD has laid on him the iniquity of us all.

Isaiah 53:3-6

The prophet Isaiah penned this scripture during the 8th century BC. Nearly seven hundred years before Jesus finally came to earth and lived these words for our benefit. Today, His Love has been poured out and we can walk fully in His joy.

We can truly forgive and love our enemies. Despite our pain. Despite our circumstances. Because we know He leads the way. A perfect teacher modeling the way for His children to truly live free. When we forgive, like Jesus, we are letting go of the sin of hating our brother or sister. And because we all essentially share our very first parents, then even my enemy is actually family. I love that modern science is catching up with God's Word on this subject. The point here being, that we all are on a level playing field. We are all human beings simply struggling together in this broken world.

Where hate and unforgiveness kills and dries up the bones, love and forgiveness bring life.

Forgiveness breathes life back into our dried-up bones. Love Himself steps in to our thinking and roots out any bitterness that was festering within. Our smiles and our laughter become real. Our eyes are no longer deadened, but alive. The Spirit of Christ permeating our core and spilling overflowingly into every area of our lives.

God's freedom is true freedom. When I forgave, I felt truly free for the first time in my life. No longer fighting to break free from a cage. The cage itself, that dark bitter place I allowed myself to reside in for far too long, simply melted away as I looked up and saw clear blue sky beckoning me to come and play.

For freedom Christ has set us free; stand firm therefore, and do not submit again to a yoke of slavery.

Galatians 5:1

`

Chapter 9:
Living Peacefully

In middle school my friends and I drew peace signs all over our school folders. We would hold up our peace signs shouting and wishing for world peace. The world is always screaming for peace. In the midst of wars and rumors of wars we desperately await the day when we will all get along. When the bad guys will stop being bad. When the goodness we think is in ourselves will finally rule.

But, world peace is not attainable. Not in our brokenness. Not in our current state. There is no goodness in our fellow man that will magically begin to rule over the darkness that currently presides. All we have to do is look around and the evidence is clear. History echoes our current cries. There is nothing new under this sun. Evil stepped in on that fateful day in the garden, and it has not left.

"The LORD saw that the wickedness of man was great in the earth, and that every intention of the thoughts of his heart was only evil continually." (Genesis 6:5)

We couldn't make it out of the very first book in God's story before we grieved our Father's heart. The Old Testament is a testament of the great contrast between man's evil intent and God's goodness alone.

"For we have already charged that all,
both Jews and Greeks, are under sin,
as it is written:

None is righteous, no, not one;
no one understands; no one seeks God.
All have turned aside;
together they have become worthless;
no one does good, not even one."

Romans 3:9-12

Can you honestly say you desperately seek God? Can you honestly say you have always done right? Even when nonbelievers and believers alike appear to be doing good, how often is it for some sort of underhanded gain? Perhaps it's hidden from our view. But God weighs the motives. Even when no one else can see, He sees the true intent of our heart. He knows when we do good for that earthly prize of human praise. He sees the pictures being snapped as the celebrities feed the poor.

What we do when we think no one is looking is the real measure of our heart.

Even at the end, the men who had promised to always be by Jesus' side ran away in fear. Our God was alone. Even the Father turned His back as Jesus took on His justified wrath for us. Jesus' friends and family had let Him down.

Checking out in a store the other day I realized I had left my wallet in the car. I yelled I would be right back to the cashier as I dashed to get it. Upon my return a young girl who was working stood there gaping at me saying she didn't think I was coming back. As we talked she admitted she had lost all faith in people and I gently reminded her, our faith should never lie in people, but God alone. He is the faithful One. The only One who is truly righteous.

When the multitude of angels announced the birth of Christ to the lowly shepherd's in the field that night, they said there was 'peace on earth.' That was two-thousand years ago. Clearly there is not, and never has been any kind of universal peace in this broken world. As always, Jesus is the answer. Jesus was the 'peace' walking on earth.

Jesus is our peace.

The peace we can find while we journey through a dry and weary land. The peace we can find when our life is ripped apart by a bullet taking our loved one's life. The peace we can find when we don't understand what the doctors are saying. The peace that doesn't make sense to a world spinning out of control.

Through the years of pain and hurt God finally brought me to the place of peace.

Jesus had set me free, just as He promised in John 8:31 when He said "…to the Jews who had believed him, 'If you abide in my word, you are truly my disciples, and you will know the truth, and the truth will set you free.'" I had felt caged since the day of my dad's murder. But as Jesus walked with me and taught me about His Love for me through His Word, I realized the door had been opened at some point in my life. All I needed to do was to step out of that lonely cage and into the Light.

My joy ran deep. I had learned to laugh through the tears of everyday life. I believed and lived out what I read in God's Word. Whether it was forgiving my dad's murderer, wholly submitting to Jesse's authority as my husband, or simply learning to rejoice in the seemingly mundane life of a stay-at-home mom. As God's Spirit filled me with His peace and joy, I found I could smile at my children and fell in love with simply being an invisible mother. Each day, I found I could live out this beautiful scripture, that is the path of true peace.

Rejoice in the Lord always;
again I will say, rejoice.

Let your reasonableness
be known to everyone.

The Lord is at hand;
do not be anxious about anything,
but in everything by prayer
and supplication with thanksgiving
let your requests be made known to God.

And the peace of God,
which surpasses all understanding
will guard your hearts
and your minds in Christ Jesus.
Philippians 4:4-7

God's peace does indeed now guard my heart and mind as I am wrapped in the arms of Jesus. As I sit at His feet and listen to the Word of Life speak. There is nothing sweeter than God's peace when we are still called to live inside our brokenness. Though we are free, we are still not completely healed. Though we are at peace, we have to stay connected to the true Vine in order to not sink in the water. And, as we are connected, we can truly live in His peace.

When we are at peace we can smile at the day ahead. Knowing we have no idea what it will truly bring. When my babies are sick. When I see the hurting around me. When I'm unable to make sense of a doctor's diagnosis. I can still be guarded by His peace. When the doctor's say I'm taking the bad news well. I am guarded by His peace. It is beyond understanding and so I don't try to explain it to them. I simply rest in His presence, knowing He is in the room with His loving arms around my shoulders. He keeps me safe in the storm.

As the trials come, and they will, we can continue to smile through our tears. My husband is in the business of helping people plan for trials that will inevitably come. His experience of dealing with people from all different walks of life has shown him this. He says you are either in a storm, just leaving a storm, or headed right for one. The night Jesus was betrayed to the authorities by a friend, He told His disciples this truth. "I have said these things to you, that in me you may have peace. In the world you will have tribulation. But take heart; I have overcome the world." (John 16:33)

He never promises an easy-street kind of life in scripture. But He does promise us this peace that truly surpasses all human reason. Life is messy and wild for this stay-at-home wife and mother with a house full of growing boys who all want to go their own way. I am not blind to the news reels of people, all made in the image of our beloved Creator, murdering one another in thought and deed. But, in the midst of the craziness, because of this peace that guards my heart and mind, I am able to still show patience and kindness. I can reach out in Love when other's may slash me with hate. I can look beyond the snide remarks of a stranger and clearly see their own hurting and pain.

I can have peace when things don't go my way. When my plans are thwarted. When my children rebel, much like I have rebelled against God. And as they grow, and the years become harder on this worn out mamma, and they become the men God has already planned for them to be, His peace will guard my heart and mind still. I do not fret and wring my hands wondering if they will make good choices. Inevitably I know they won't. Not always. But God's peace tells me it is in His loving hands, so I close my eyes and rest, with a smile curving on my lips. Jesus slept in the midst of the storm. We can too, if we know He is holding our hand.

God's peace guards us when we are being tossed in the waves and the storm seems never to let up. We have to remember Jesus is in the boat with us. The Creator of heaven and earth. Within our grasp. And as we wake Him and cry out to him in our fear, He faithfully saves us and calms the storm within. He takes away the unnecessary panic and gives us the gift of His everlasting peace.

In peace
I will both lie down and sleep:
For you alone, O Lord,
make me dwell in safety.
Psalm 4:8

Chapter 10:
Turn

When John the Baptist came preaching repentance, he was preparing the way for Jesus. Preparing the hearts of the people to first understand their sin, and then learn how to turn away from that sin. It is always perplexing to think of this. That John did not come beside people timidly and say, "Now let's ask Jesus to come into your heart."

No, he first clearly pointed out their sin.

That is what confused me for much of my life. As a girl I didn't understand my personal sin. And as an adult I meet people all the time who sincerely believe they are a good person. And a good person does not need to be saved. A good person can get to heaven on their own. A good person can not comprehend the need to ask some strange man who lived and died two-thousand years ago to come into their heart.

So, how does a person, who seemingly lives a good life, come to the place of seeing their sin?

Again, we must dig into the Word of God. And ask the hard questions. What does He say? What are His standards of goodness and why should we care?

The law of God confuses most in our modern culture. Laws are linked to restrictions. And no one likes the idea of being restricted. Of feeling caged. We have the desire to live without chains. Without the weight of boring rules and regulations. And, as with everything else in our brokenness, we stand ready to break any law that leaves us feeling chained.

In our country laws are constantly changing. And so, there seems to be a sense of whatever feels right must be right. What's right for me is good and what's right for you is good, too. God's law, however, never changes. It was in the beginning and it will be so in the end. As confusing as reading God's law can be for most, I've noticed there is this mysterious moral compass already written on the heart of every man, woman and child, though we try hard to fight it.

I've never met someone who would say they believe murder isn't wrong. I've never met someone who would say it feels great when their spouse or significant other betrays their trust. I've never met someone who would say they enjoy when a thief breaks in and steals everything they own. Somehow there is a sense of morality woven deep into our core being. I have witnessed the youngest of children become ferociously angry over an injustice that has occurred. When my twins steal from each other the screaming and gnashing of teeth is a sight to behold. When I promise something to my older kids, and then that promise is not fulfilled, they feel the injustice deeply.

Yes, we all have the law of God written on our hearts. No matter how much we fight it, there is much evidence that our Creator put His mark on His creation. And as He walked the earth among His creation we found His standards to be even higher than we first understood in the law. Jesus says if we hate; we have murdered. If we look; we have committed adultery. If we covet; we have stolen. Man may look at his outward appearance and say he is doing pretty good. But, God sees our heart. He knows our thoughts and deeds we try to hide. As Adam and Eve hid, so do we. And, as the Father knew where they were and what they had done, He knows what we do in secret, too.

If we are honest, we know we have this moral compass intricately woven into who we are.

Ultimately though, our moral compass will only take us so far. And our Father knew that as well. That is why He wrote us this beautiful love letter. The Word of God. I have a letter my dad wrote to us girls while he sat in a prison cell. It's framed and hanging on the wall where I get ready in the mornings. I love to see that letter. My dad wrote it when I was very young, but the words still describe who I want to be. He said I was pure and bright as my name implied. He said I had a curiosity and willingness to learn about everything around me. Indeed, I want to be those things. I want to be pure. I want to be bright and walk in the Light always. And I want to keep learning about God's awe-inspiring creation until the day He takes me away from here.

At the end of my dad's letter he pleads with us not to forget him. As he sat alone behind those cold bars I can only imagine how he felt thinking of the family he loved. Hoping we hadn't forgotten all about him. And, of course, we couldn't then and won't now. He will forever be a part of who I am. A part of my life.

Now, how much more amazing is my Heavenly Father's love letter written with the utmost care to His beloved children. His children who were lost from Him in the garden. His children who ran from Him and fought against Him. His delight, stumbling around in darkness instead of His radiant Light.

God's love letter also pleads with His children not to forget Him. He pleads with us to believe that He knows what is best, even when it doesn't make sense to us. He disciplines us. Loves us. Cares for us. He tells us His story. How He came from far away to rescue us. How He endured torture and ran to take our place on the chopping block that we so deserved.

What a disgrace to my dad's memory if I simply tossed aside that letter written to me out of love all those years ago. What a much bigger disgrace when we disregard God's love letter.

And there lies our sin.

When we are not willing to even read, and certainly not obey, this beautiful love letter. The Word of God. His perfect law that protects us from our own destruction. That leads us. Guides us. Lifts us back into communion with the Creator of the universe.

And the sad truth is that none of us really want that. Adam and Eve essentially ate the one thing they couldn't have because they wanted to be God. When we refuse to listen and obey then we too are saying we want to be God. And that is sin. You can argue with me until you are blue in the face. But, as Job discovered through his many trials, and I have discovered in mine, we are not the Creator. I was not there in the beginning when He created. I do not know how He made everything out of nothing. And so, I can choose to believe He is who He says He is, or I can choose to go my own way and hope I'm a good enough person.

I often tell my boys that God did not want robots. He wanted a beautiful family. Just as I know my boys will go their own way and make up their own mind, God knew we would, too. And, thankfully, He pursues us still. I was His faithless daughter for a long time. But He did not stop until I was found and turned back to Him. He did not force my love. As I can't force my own children to love me. But, I pursue them when they try to hide. I give them space when I know that's what they need. But I never leave. I wait and watch and when they are ready I pursue some more. Our Father is relentlessly in love with us.

My sin of running away from Him. My sin of not listening to Him and thinking I knew best. That is the ultimate sin. Thinking I know more than the Great I AM. Thinking that I didn't need the One who made me and knows me best.

After we see our sin what do we do?

John told us to repent. To turn. To get on a new path. The path that leads to life. In Luke chapter three, John helped the people begin to see what it looked like to repent when "the crowds asked him,

'What shall we do?' And he answered them, 'Whoever has two tunics is to share with him who has none, and whoever has food is to do likewise.'" (Luke 3:10-11)

The tax collectors who were professing faith also wanted to know what it looked like for them to repent and John told them plainly, "Collect no more [taxes] than you are authorized to do." (Luke 3:13) In other words, don't cheat people in business dealings.

The Roman soldiers who were coming to faith also wanted to know what they needed to do to live a repentant life and once again John made it crystal clear. He told them 'not to extort money from anyone by threats or by false accusation and be content with your wages.' (Luke 3:14) These soldiers occupying Judea could easily use their power to terrify the people into doing whatever they wanted. Repenting and turning from that sin was simple. Don't do it. Don't take advantage of others even when you have the opportunity.

Amazingly God speaks plainly in His word regarding our sin and how to repent and live the life He is calling us to. There is no secret code we have to unlock. It's sad to sit in a church bible study and hear the religious super stars, the Pharisees of our day, bickering over what a particular passage actually means. They pick at it and pull it apart to a point beyond recognition and conclude that God is confusing.

God is not confusing. His ways are higher than our ways. And, though we may never fully comprehend the beautiful complexities of His ways, when it comes to how He is calling us to live on this earth, when it comes to the basics of repentance and the gospel, He couldn't be clearer. Jesus spoke very plainly to the people. He didn't speak above their heads to show off how smart He was. And, I'm pretty sure He was the smartest person who ever lived. After all, He created the universe we spend a lifetime studying and never fully understanding.

Jesus broke it down and told them parables. The only reason scripture says the masses didn't comprehend at that time was because it was God's plan so that Jesus could die on the cross. When the story was complete. When He said those beautiful, long awaited words, "It is finished," then the love letter could be completed and the scales were able to fall from our eyes. (John 19:30)

Just a few short years after Jesus completed His task of reuniting us to the Father, the apostle Paul would write to the church in Ephesus explaining this great truth and mystery.

"And you were dead
in the trespasses and sins
in which you once walked,
following the course of this world,

following the prince of the power of the air,
the spirit that is now at work
in the sons of disobedience —

among whom we all once lived
in the passions of our flesh,
carrying out the desires of the body
and the mind,

and were by nature
children of wrath,
like the rest of mankind."

Ephesians 2:1-3

Paul would go on to explain how the mysteries of God, regarding the gospel, have been finally revealed to us all in these last days. Both to Jews and Greeks.

In His love letter to us, the bible, He shows us our sin and how to turn from it. The mystery of His unyielding love is explained fully. And today we can take great comfort in knowing the Creator of the universe has kept His love letter in tack, despite the imperfections of humans. He would not have gone through the trouble of writing us a love letter over the course of thousands of years to simply let that love letter become distorted in any way. We can trust His supremacy and sovereignty in this, as well as everything else.

Paul also told the body of Christ living in Ephesus these words, this timeless truth that still holds the same weight for those of us who are Christians today. He wrote:

"...the mystery of Christ,
which was not made known
to the sons of men in other generations
as it has now been revealed
to his holy apostles and prophets by the Spirit.

This mystery is that the Gentiles are fellow heirs,
members of the same body,
and partakers of the promise
in Christ Jesus through the gospel."
Ephesians 3:4-6

We, the Gentile groups, the people in this world not of physical Jewish descent, have now been grafted in and adopted as sons and daughters by the King of the universe. Jews and Gentiles alike can believe in this God-Man, Jesus Christ, the Messiah who saves us from our own destruction, and actually become a part of God's family.

How I respond to this is everything.

Do I allow other Christians to pat me on the back, as we chuckle together that we're not perfect, but that God loves us anyway? Do I allow other women to speak ill of my husband and make me feel inferior if I am subject to his authority over my life? Do I treat my beloved children with contempt when no one is looking?

Do I toss the Word aside, possibly even forgetting it in the floor-board of my truck all week, only to pick it up, dust it off and smile as I walk into that church building on Sunday morning?

What are my hidden actions when I think no one is looking?

None of us are perfect. Deep down our moral compass tells us this truth. That is why Jesus had to come. He had to come save us because we do need to be saved.

And when our eyes are open to this fact, then John tells us to simply repent. Turn. Veer off the current course we are on that leads to destruction and get on the new path that leads to life.

And what does this look like in today's world?

True repentance is simply taking God at His Word. No excuses. Just taking Him at His Word.

And if we don't know what His Word says, then a great place to start is pulling it off your shelf, wiping off the cobwebs, and reading it.

But, don't take my word for it. Or anyone else's. Pick it up for yourself. In a quiet room where only God can see you. And in the wonderful stillness of that moment, His Words may just start to leap of those beautiful pages. Living Words coming to life right before your eyes. Speaking life and pouring love deep into the deepest recesses of your soul.

Don't be intimidated by not knowing where to start. His entire love letter, all sixty-six books of it, is truly a treasure that lovingly points us to Him.

Just start at the beginning. He'll take it from there.

"Come to Me,
all who labor and are heavy laden,
and I will give you rest.

Take My yoke upon you,
and learn from Me,
for I am gentle and lowly in heart,
and you will find rest for your souls.

For my yoke is easy,
and my burden is light."

Matthew 11:28-30

Chapter 11: Redemption

As a young college-student I walked timidly, rebelliously into the small, newly opened Christian bookstore in my hometown on a rare weekend visit. Up until that point the only bible I had come into contact with was the King James version. That little country church I faithfully attended during my high school years taught me the new versions were watered down and could not be trusted. We lived in fear of the changing world. In fear of what we couldn't understand. Deep rooted tradition was our stronghold.

But there I was, rebelling, starving for His Word. Thirsting for something more. Knowing there was intimacy behind the code of writing I just couldn't wrap my mind around. As I had sat in an English class surrounded by other 19-year-olds, discussing, dissecting Shakespeare, it suddenly dawned on me that this is how I felt as I stumbled through scripture. I couldn't just read and allow the words to penetrate my core when I was constantly unraveling this seemingly mysterious coded message.

So, I decided to rebel against tradition. I wasn't being malicious. I was simply starving to death.

The first bible I bought for myself was the New American Standard version. It read exactly like I spoke. I felt like I finally had the Word of God in my own language, and as I began to look and see and understand those seemingly forbidden words, my world finally began to change.

Fear is a strange thing. Fear is paralyzing. It plays tricks on us and threatens us. Fear is not from God. God is Love. And His perfect love casts out fear. His perfect love teaches me to never live in fear. As I see His power and justice and love, I can know, and take great comfort in simply living in awe and reverence of Him.

Jesus said, "…have no fear of them, for nothing is covered that will not be revealed, or hidden that will not be known. What I tell you in the dark, say in the light, and what you hear whispered, proclaim on the housetops. And do not fear those who kill the body but cannot kill the soul. Rather fear him who can destroy both soul and body in hell." (Matthew 10:26-28)

I have no fear of 'them.' Whomever 'them' may be. That is how I can stand and speak kindly to a man in a crowded coffee shop when others in my small town tell me to stay away because I should be terrified of him. That is how I can testify for my best friend when she is trying to escape an abusive situation that seems overwhelming and incredibly terrifying. If I feel myself becoming paralyzed with very real fear, when the enemy is at hand, I am able stand and fight for the truth only when I remember Jesus's words.

I choose to walk out my faith in the One who promises to be with me even in the shadow of death. He 'prepare[s] a table before me in the presence of my enemies,' but I will not fear them. (Psalm 23:5)

I can pray for them and love them with this power from the God who loved me and pursued me when I was still His enemy. "But I say to you, love your enemies and pray for those who persecute you, so that you may be sons of your Father who is in heaven. For He makes His sun rise on the evil and on the good and sends rain on the just and the unjust. For if you love those who love you, what reward do you have?" (Matthew 5:44-46)

Some people are easy to love. But when the gospel penetrates our lives we begin to understand the power and beauty of truly loving our enemies. The people that are hard to love. We can love them only when we begin to see just how unlovable we were when Christ chose to love us.

The Samaritans were enemies of the Jews for as long as anyone could remember. They hated the Jews and the Jews hated them. When Jesus started telling them to love these people, who had always been a true enemy, they were understandably perplexed. But, He was revealing God's great mystery. The beauty of the greatest love story of all time. That's what the bible is. A love story of a Father relentlessly loving His family.

Recently, I heard a preacher expound on a familiar story honing in on this love story. Sometimes I forget the true gospel. Sometimes I can become overwhelmed by the greatness of my sin. When I worry if I'm not doing enough. When I become disconnected from the Vine that feeds me. The gospel can become blurry in the busyness of trying.

Once again, Jesus comes to my rescue. He gently slips His scarred hand in mine and sits with me. He directs my attention back to Him.

As the preacher told us where to turn in our bible's I almost, pridefully tuned him out.

Luke chapter 10 starting in verse 25. Yes, I know this story. The Good Samaritan. I've heard it a thousand times. As he read and lectured, my mind wandered, rolling the familiar parable over in my own head. I knew what he would say. I'm going to feel guilty for not doing more. I will plead with my husband that we should do more and he will argue that our lives are too hectic right now to over-extend ourselves further. My husband would remind me I'm on modified bedrest during this high-risk pregnancy, but even then, I knew I would still feel worthless and unworthy because I can't currently *do* anything for the gospel.

I wasn't in the mood to hear this sermon on serving more.

But, just as the pity-party in my head was really revving up, Jesus Himself nudged me to sit up and pay attention to the preacher's words…

"A man was going down from Jerusalem to Jericho,
and he fell among robbers,
who stripped him and beat him and departed,
leaving him half dead.

Now by chance a priest was going down that road,
and when he saw him he passed by on the other side.

So, like-wise a Levite,
when he came to the place and saw him,
passed by on the other side.

But a Samaritan [his enemy],
as he journeyed, came to where he was,
and when he saw him, he had compassion.

He went to him and bound up his wounds,
pouring on oil and wine.
Then he set him on his own animal
and brought him to an inn and took care of him.

And the next day he took out two denarii
[two days-worth of his wages]
and gave them to the innkeeper, saying,

'Take care of him, and whatever more you spend,
I will repay you when I come back.'"

Luke 10:30-35

I had heard sermons on this passage of scripture a hundred times before. I thought I knew it well. But God's Word is living and breathing. If we allow it to it will continue to grow us and mold us as long as we are living and breathing.

What I didn't see in this moment was exactly what Jesus knew I needed to hear. To be reminded of. When the preacher asked who we identified with the most I quickly knew I was too much like the priest and the Levite. Passing by on the other side. Seeing my enemy and ducking behind a wall. Seeing my enemy, broken and hurting. Desperately needing a Savior. Yet, too often I had chosen to ignore the hurting and pass by on the opposite side of the street. Not wanting to get involved, and then beating myself up about it later.

As my thoughts rattled on into self-loathing the preacher finally concluded with the life-giving words I had allowed myself to forget for that one sinful moment. He simply said we are the man beaten and lying in the ditch half-dead.

Jesus. Is. Our. Good. Samaritan.

Yes! How do I ever forget this? *The gospel. The Good News.* The life-changing good news that is the answer to our brokenness.

We left God's beautiful city and went on our way, thinking we knew what was best. And when this world beat us up beyond recognition, leaving us half-dead and broken beyond repair, Jesus saw us and had compassion. He crossed the road and got involved. He picked us up and carried us to safety. He paid for us and promised to cover whatever expense we incur, as we are made well, and continue to get lost in the darkness of our world.

Religion can not save us. The priest saw us but passed by. The law can not save us. The Levite saw us but passed by. Only the Good Samaritan, God's Love wrapped in flesh, Jesus Himself, can save us. He saw His enemy in need and acted out of pure love and compassion. Only Jesus can be our perfect neighbor who truly loves us and cares for us. The rest of us will always fall short of that mark. In our trying we fall short. Selfishness creeps in. But, Jesus, our Good Samaritan, has thankfully journeyed our way.

***

When I am reminded of the beautiful, life-giving gospel, I can exhale and feel the freedom once again. The freedom His love gives me when I've stubbornly stumbled back into my cage. The freedom to love and be loved. The freedom to not try.

When I am free I can listen joyfully to the wisdom of my own husband. After all these years I still marvel at Jesse. How he gently leads me, *just like Jesus leads His own bride*. And this is the true mystery of marriage. Marriage is wrapped up in the gospel.

'Wives submit to your own husbands, as to the Lord. For the husband is the head of the wife even as Christ is the head of the church, his body, and is himself its Savior. Now as the church submits to Christ, so also wives should submit in everything to their husbands.' (Ephesians 5:22-24)

'Older women…teach what is good, and so train the young women to love…and [be] submissive to their own husbands, that the word of God may not be reviled.' Titus 2:3-5 (paraphrased)

'Likewise, wives, be subject to your own husbands…[and] let your adorning be the hidden person of the heart with the imperishable beauty of a gentle and quiet spirit, which in God's sight is very precious. For this is how the holy women who hoped in God used to adorn themselves, by submitting to their own husbands, as Sarah obeyed Abraham, calling him lord. And you are her children, if you do good and do not fear anything that is frightening.'
1 Peter 3:1-6 (paraphrased)

God knows, because of what happened when Eve sinned back in the garden, that obeying our husbands in this day and age can be incredibly frightening. But, He tells us not to succumb to ungodly fear. I can imagine the fear Sarah must have felt when her husband told her that they would be packing up and leaving everything they had ever known. Her home and I'm sure her comfort. There is no record of her complaints. Only scripture confirming she obeyed her husband in everything because God was not only the God of Abraham, but also, the God of Sarah. And in her submitting she was immensely blessed.

The mystery of marriage is the mystery of Christ and His church, His bride. Ephesians chapter five concludes with taking a sudden turn from giving us every-day practical marriage advice, to spinning it into what God ultimately created marriage for.

"'Therefore, a man shall leave his father and mother and hold fast to his wife and the two shall become one flesh.' This mystery is profound, and I am saying that it refers to Christ and the church." (Ephesians 5:31-32)

Jesus left His Father to cleave to His wife, the church. The church is not an institution or a building. The church is a living, breathing organism. An organic underground movement across our globe. Jesus breathing life into this body, His bride. Saving us, caring for us, drawing us over and over again to Himself. And in His pursuit and love for us we, His bride, are finding our joy and peace in His presence alone.

And the last line of the hard to chew on 'marriage' chapter sums it all up with this: 'However, let each one of you love his wife as himself, and let the wife see that she respects her husband.' (Ephesians 5:33)

Jesus loves the church, His body and His bride, just as if taking care of His own. Within the context of the covenant of marriage, God is calling on men to have this unwavering love for their own wives.

And we the church, billions of Jesus-followers all over the planet, who submit to the authority and teaching of Christ would never dream of disobeying His words because He is our Lord. With this same unyielding devotion that the church shows Christ, He tells us who are wives to respect, submit, obey and love our own husbands.

Why?

Because biblical marriage is meant to be a beautiful representation of our relationship with Jesus.

As Jesus is the head of the church, so Jesse is the head of me. And the more I wholeheartedly follow the command's I see in the Word that leads to abundant life, the more Jesse loves me and treats me with the most tender care. And as I lean in to my husband's wisdom and authority over me, I find my communion with God goes deeper still.

As I am deeply rooted in God's love and connected to His Word, I wake with thoughts of serving and loving Jesse. My nearest neighbor. If my plans are disrupted in order to help him in some way, then I can rest in knowing my heavenly Father has called and created me for this. Jesus says to 'go and do likewise' at the end of the Good Samaritan story. And only after allowing the beauty of His gospel to truly penetrate my core, then I find I can truly love and serve my neighbor.

And God shows me who my closest neighbors are and that I am to start there. My husband is first. Always. Then I see our children. Do I stop and pay attention to them, or do I pass by in the busyness of my day?

Following my husband and our small children, my next 'neighbor' is whomever the Lord puts in front of me as I walk hand in hand with Him throughout my day.

When a close friend calls because she needs to talk, do I really listen and bear her burdens as my own? When I'm minding my own business and the Holy Spirit lays someone on my heart, do I put my agenda on hold as I stop and pray and then pick up the phone to call and offer what I can?

Am I too busy for the person God puts right in front of me?

Am I the priest trying to get to where he is going? Building church 'buildings' or connecting with the hurting around me? Am I the Levite, one who knows the law better than most, and yet has not allowed the gospel to seep into his heart?

How has the gospel changed me?

It's my quiet daily life behind closed doors that show my change. As His fruit manifests deep and slowly becomes my fruit. I can show patience with my children and handle their tiny souls ever so gently. His love, joy and peace keep my brokenness bound and I begin to be kinder to my husband. I am capable of showing goodness to a stranger in need by sharing what I have, expecting nothing in return. I am a faithful friend. And when the hate of this world attacks with full force, I can turn the other cheek with pure self-control.

But the fruit of the Spirit is love, joy, peace,
patience, kindness, goodness, faithfulness, gentleness, self-control;
against such things there is no law.
Galatians 5:22-23

Chapter 12:
The End

"How long will you go here and there,
O faithless daughter?

For the LORD has created a new thing in the earth —
A woman will encompass a man."

Jeremiah 31:22

Jesus brought me back to Himself when He first showed me Jeremiah 31:22 all those years ago. Trying to stay warm in the frozen north, huddled in that tiny basement apartment, God was patient with me. He is still patient with me, as He thankfully is with all of us. I'm not sure that in this lifetime we can perfectly, truly comprehend the depths nor heights of His love for us. But the apostle Paul prayed that we would. And so, maybe we will. At times I have a slight glimpse, and in those moments of wonder, I am breathlessly mesmerized by Him.

I know now that the words of Jeremiah 31:22 were not just talking about me and my husband. But, Christ and His church. Jesus. Surrounded by His church, His bride, His people. The Father finally, eternally back in right relationship with His creation that He has always loved and will always fight for.

Living redeemed means the once great mystery of the gospel, God's perfect love and sacrifice for us, is fully made known to me. I am no longer confused by the dirtiness of this world. The dirtiness in me. I can read the bible and not allow the filthiness I see there to confuse me. The bible is not full of good people and bad people who we should try or try not to emulate. It is the love story of a great King who wants His family back. And He finds us. He fights for us. He loves us. Despite the grime we have been wallowing in since the beginning of time.

As He journeyed through His creation, looking for His children, He found me, His faithless, broken daughter in the ditch. He picked me up, wiped off the dirt and cleaned my wounds. He put the pieces of me back together and expertly bound up my broken heart.

And even now, though I am clean, if I stumble and scrape my knee I know to run straight to my Father and he will kiss my wounds and make them better. He will love me through the storm.

I no longer wonder at the dirtiness of others. I no longer wonder at the mistakes of my dad, as he may have wondered at the mistakes of his dad, who may have wondered at the mistakes of his dad, and on and on. As I sit and listen and learn while the preacher expounds on God's Word, I don't have to sit and wonder at the imperfect pastor's imperfections.

Jesus holds up the mirror and I can see my own reflection for what it is. My own brokenness. My deep scars. But then, He puts down the mirror and my eyes are able to focus on Him. His goodness and mercy and love and sacrifice. I let His perfect love cast out all my fear and fully penetrate my core.

I smile. I laugh. I sing. Finally understanding that when the Father looks at me, His faithless daughter, He doesn't see the filth or the faithlessness anymore. He only sees the righteous One sitting with me. Jesus, the only righteous One, holding me close and covering me with His righteousness. And as we sit together, He slips me a gift. The beautiful gift of faith. Because even that is a gift from the Father who only gives good gifts to His beloved children.

God knows we are all dirty because we were born into a grimy, filthy world. A world that was broken long ago. That is why He had to come down to where we were. We were too dirty to climb back up to Him.

My children often speak ill of Adam and Eve. They want to know why they couldn't just get it right. Why they had to eat the one thing they couldn't have. When this world hurts we are always looking for someone to blame. But the truth is, and I am forever attempting to gently teach this to my own little sinners, that we all would have blown it if we were in our first parents' place. None of us can ever just seem to get it right. The sanctification process is long and hard. Harder than most of us would like to admit. Just when I start to look around and allow myself to wonder at another's imperfections, the mirror rears its ugly self, and I realize that dirty, imperfect person staring out at me is, well...me.

Jesus is the only Person who came into this filthy world and managed to stay clean. His heart stayed pure. His love stayed one with the Father. Then He willingly took my deserved punishment and set me free.

How the enemy wants me to forget that. Because when I forget it, I willingly walk back into my cage and stop loving others. But, if I keep my eyes on Jesus, the God-Man who died in my place, then I am free indeed.

Free to walk through this life loving my enemy and praying for those who hurt me. Free to simply live and pass the mantel to the next generation. Long before me and long after me there will remain one constant: Jesus.

***

Jesus. The beginning and the end. Who knitted me together and knows me better than I know myself. He was the only One in the beginning. Creating. Loving. Shining. And so, He will be in the very end. His glory. There for all to see.

The gospel, this Good News, allows us to live free here in our brokenness. We have true joy and peace that surpasses all understanding. Yet, we are still broke. There is a day we are looking forward to. When this life ends and eternity begins. The end becomes the beginning. Our new beginning.

The gospel has saved me from myself. The gospel allows me to see past my fear and hold fast to my Savior while we travel through the storm. Yet, even though I now have the power to forgive my enemies, the hurt is still here. I am not bitter or angry, but the tears still come. I am not fearful of man, but the pain is very real.

We do not simply get over losing a loved one. And Jesus does not expect us to suck it up and deal with it. He holds us and loves us as we are brought to our knees shaking from the deep grief, promising to make it all right in the end. Promising to carry us when we are crushed and beaten down, and to give us the strength we need to carry on. To persevere. To bear good fruit and to continue walking through this life able and willing to love. Able to live a life pleasing to Him.

I once sat with a kind old man at the end of his days. He had lived a long earthly life and seen a lot. Fought in wars. Traveled. Married. Raised children. Lived. But, as he lay there so close to his ending and spoke with me, his mind drifted to the memory of his little sister who had died as a child. She was so young he reflected. He still missed her. After a lifetime without her. He still missed her. His eyes filled with tears at the thought of her and the pain came rushing in again.

Then he looked at me and wondered why someone like me was wasting my time at the bedside of an old dying man. I wanted to tell him how much I loved him. A stranger to me, but not to Jesus. To tell him his tears were precious and caught and treasured by a Father who loves him. But, the poetic words didn't come and all I could do was smile into the eyes of this dear child of God and love him quietly in his pain.

How often do I hear people trying to shrug off death and make light of something incredibly heavy? I saw a woman and heard her ninety-nine-year-old mother had just passed away. As we stood there on the busy street I gave her permission in my compassion to grieve the loss of her dear mom. She was stunned and immensely grateful that I treated her pain with care. Instead of celebrating that her mother had lived so long, and expecting her to be glad, I held her hand as Jesus would and allowed her to cry.

Death is always sad. No matter how long or how short. It is gut-wrenchingly sad because it reminds us of our sin and brokenness. Without our first parents sinning in the garden, death would not be a part of our vocabulary. We are eternal beings, trapped in a broken world.

"Then I saw a new heaven and a new earth,
for the first heaven and the first earth
had passed away,
and the sea was no more.

And I saw the holy city, new Jerusalem,
coming down out of heaven from God,
prepared as a bride adorned for her husband.

And I heard a loud voice from the throne saying,
'Behold, the dwelling place of God is with man.

He will dwell with them,
and they will be his people,
and God himself will be with them
as their God.

He will wipe away every tear from their eyes,
and death shall be no more,
neither shall there be mourning,
nor crying, nor pain anymore,
for the former things have passed away.'"
Revelation 21:1-4

Our brokenness is still very real here. Until Jesus comes again and finally makes all things new I will still be crushed by the deep pain of my dad's unsolved murder. Jesus holds me and comforts me. My husband holds me and comforts me, too.

Maybe I will see my dad when I get to the other side. My daddy who is really gone. Never to be seen on this earth again. Ripped away. Taken in an instant. The authorities later told us that they did indeed offer him witness protection, but he refused it without hesitation. They said he told them he didn't want to ruin our lives and force us to live on the run because of his mistakes. He wanted us, his beloved family, to live free.

I could not live in that freedom, until I met Christ.

And as I walk into the new heaven and the new earth I might see my dad, hopefully smiling and laughing, just as I remember him. I might see all the loved ones I've lost and rejoice in meeting them again.

187

But, I won't be able to help looking past them in that moment. I will be looking for Him. And as our eyes meet I will run to Him. I will fall at His feet and worship. When I finally look up there will be this God-Man, the Man of Sorrows Himself, my Rescuer, my Lord and my friend, looking into my eyes. Smiling at me. And as I climb up into His lap and let him wrap me in His loving arms once and for all, I will know I am finally home.

And so, we look heavenward. Knowing God always keeps His promises. Smiling in the here and now. Patiently waiting on the Father to lovingly clean up our mess. We wait and look for our coming Savior as we love our neighbor. As we share this beautiful story of the Prince come to rescue His bride. The greatest love story of all time.

After my grandmother died, I walked through the graveyard remembering those you had come and gone long before me. Tucked away in the hills of north Georgia lay my grandparents, and great-grandparents and great-great grandparents on my mother's side.

Faithful, hardworking farmers. On one of the oldest tombstones of my late family member the epitaph simply read, 'he loved his bible.'

"That's what I want on my grave-stone," I had told my mom, as we stood in awe of this man's faithfulness. That is what I want my life and death to point to. God. And God alone. My story pointing to His. He was with me in my beginning and will be with me in my end. The alpha and omega. The beginning and the end Himself. The maker of heaven and earth. Come down to save His beloved children.

And as I rest in the boat and pass through this great storm, I know when I finally close my eyes for the last time, I will awake to see that glorious day. A new dawn. While we wait for that day, we can sing and dance in the rain. We can smile and laugh and love. Even as I sit feeling this baby growing inside of me not knowing what tomorrow will bring. Feeling the deep pain as I sit in the doctor's office watching this beautiful baby boy kick and flip and dance in my womb where God expertly knitted him together. The pain is great when they tell me this little life may not make it because my body is not cooperating.

But the joy is greater still.

And I can smile through my tears until the Lord calls us to our new home. A home unbroken. Perfect. Beyond anything we can possibly imagine.

I tell my children not to weep and mourn for their mom too much. Because when my end comes, whenever God has foreordained for that to be, it will really be my new beginning. I will be in the arms of Jesus, and He will be wiping away my very last tear.

He is there preparing our new home right now as we pass through the storm. And, He is coming back to lead the way, for those of us He has called according to His good purpose. We can look heavenward smiling,

with true peace and joy deeply rooted in our hearts,
while we wait and listen and obey His Word of Life.

"And behold,
I am coming soon.

Blessed is the one
who keeps the words
of the prophesy of this book."

Revelation 22:7

He says we are blessed if we keep His Word.
His Word that shows us how to love and be loved. We
are blessed because He really is coming back. And He
will make all things that are dreadfully wrong, right.

He tarries now for just a little while so that other's may hear of Him. Not wanting any to perish.

But, at the perfect time, He will come back to the world we broke. He will restore us completely and finally make all things new. I don't know when. I just know it will be soon. And I have hope in that. I have hope in Him. And my joy is complete as I wait for His return. For Jesus, the Creator of this universe, has promised. And He always keeps His promises.

Now to him who is able
to keep you from stumbling

and to present you blameless
before the presence of his glory
with great joy,

to the only God, our Savior,
through Jesus Christ our Lord,

be glory, majesty, dominion, and authority,
before all time and now and forever.
Amen.

Jude 24-25

Soli Deo Gloria!

The End.

About the Author

CJP Navarro is still living in the season of being a 'young' Titus 2 woman. Loving and being loved by her Creator and her blessings around her. Married to her college sweetheart, Jesse, and mother to her four little men in training, with a fifth son on the way. They live near Asheville, NC.

Though the author loves to write, this is technically not her season to do so. Most days you may catch a blurred glimpse of her speeding by as she runs her boys to soccer and wherever else they need to go; or simply chasing her hilarious twin toddler's around the house, dodging large piles of laundry and laughing out loud at the ridiculousness and beauty that is her life.

You can contact her at:

cjpnavarro@gmail.com

Scripture quotes:

The Widow's ~~Mite~~ *Might*

A Study Through Proverbs 31

Written by: CJP Navarro

Chapter 1:

Meet Joan

Joan in Hebrew means 'heroine' and 'God-loving.' It is comical how someone's name can fit them so well. My mother has always been my hero. That may sound like such a cliché, but it's true.

As a very young child my dad was my hero. But when he died, I watched my thirty-seven-year-old widowed mother come to life in a way that I hope words can explain. Her faithfulness in taking care of us kids is overwhelming to ponder. I can't get over her strong resolve and stubbornness to never give up. No one came to our rescue. No one, but my mom. She was our rock. She kept us going when we were paralyzed with fear. She fought for us when we strayed onto dark paths. She worked long hours with a smile on her face. She helped those in need, though our need was just as great. She was our biggest fan and loudest cheerleader. She was faithful for as long as we needed her.

Her life has been marked with great suffering. Yet, her light shines brighter still. Her smile is famously radiant with clear blue eyes that really do sparkle. Now in her sixties she looks as youthful as ever. Strangers open-up to her and can't get enough. They are drawn to her light like a moth to a flame. Children run to her to be kissed and cuddled. Knowing there is safety in her arms. Disgruntled adults melt in her presence and depart as life-long friends. Her children rise up and call her blessed. She is a walking, breathing, 'Proverbs 31 Woman' in the flesh.

An excellent wife who can find?
She is far more precious than jewels.
The heart of her husband trusts in her,
and he will have no lack of gain.

She does him good, and not harm,
all the days of her life.

She seeks wool and flax,
and works with willing hands.
She is like the ships of the merchant;
she brings her food from afar.

She rises while it is yet night
and provides food for her household
and portions for her maidens.

She considers a field and buys it;
with the fruit of her hands she plants a vineyard.

She dresses herself with strength
and makes her arms strong.

She perceives that her merchandise is profitable.
Her lamp does not go out at night.
She puts her hands to the distaff,
and her hands hold the spindle.

She opens her hand to the poor
and reaches out her hands to the needy.
She is not afraid of snow for her household,
for all her household are clothed in scarlet.
She makes bed coverings for herself;
her clothing is fine linen and purple.

Her husband is known in the gates
when he sits among the elders of the land.
She makes linen garments and sells them;
she delivers sashes to the merchant.

Strength and dignity are her clothing,
and she laughs at the time to come.

She opens her mouth with wisdom,
and the teaching of kindness is on her tongue.
She looks well to the ways of her household
and does not eat the bread of idleness.

Her children rise up and call her blessed;
her husband also, and he praises her;

"Many women have done excellently,
but you surpass them all."

Charm is deceitful, and beauty is vain,
but a woman who fears the LORD is to be praised.
Give her of the fruit of her hands,
and let her works praise her in the gates.
Proverbs 31:10-31

My mom epitomizes the infamous 'Proverbs 31 Woman'. As an adult I now marvel at her and wonder about her story. This skinny, malnourished country girl who grew up to marry a rolling-stone that she barely knew. This painfully shy, incredibly beautiful, and extremely intelligent girl who has become our town jewel. This is the widow Jesus saw in the temple that day. The widow who faithfully, quietly put in her two mites barely worth a penny. Yet, Jesus noticed just how big her sacrifice really was. And He blessed her for it.

But, before the blessing came the storm. Before the woman we see today there was heart-ache beyond belief.

That last night together was sweet. Life had been hard. Mistakes had been made and forgiveness needed to be asked. By both husband and wife. They wanted to make up. They wanted to continue. To persevere and raise their growing family together. To put the pieces back together. That night they said they were sorry. They made up. Like a thousand couples before them. Two souls being molded into one in the midst of a broken world. The last few years had been hard for Joan. How could she know the next few would prove even harder? The hopeful couple that night didn't know it would be their last.

The morning came, and Joan became our young widow to a murdered husband.

Tom stood in his upstairs bathroom taking his last toke as he stared into the woods beyond the house; Joan made pancakes downstairs. She smiled as Tom came downstairs and sat down to eat his breakfast. Her eyes full of joy as she watched him laughing with their only son, who was just over three. Tom's pride and joy. How sweet it was to see the proud, young daddy sharing hot pancakes with his smiling toddler.

He had told Joan how much he wanted a son even before their wedding day. Ironically, that son didn't come until after Tom was first arrested for drug-trafficking. The beginning of the end for him. True joy in having his boy, shadowed by too many mistakes catching up at once. Still, the joy was there for Tom and Joan she reflected that morning. Despite the cloud they couldn't get away from, there was laughter and joy. Young dad and his son laughed together now, sharing pancakes. Tom looking as handsome as ever in the light blue sweater she had found recently at a local thrift store in her frugality.

When Tom finally jumped up to leave he kissed his boy, his 5-month-old daughter, his beautiful trophy wife, nodded a good-bye to his mother-in-law and grabbed his crutches. Their three older daughters already gone to school. Joan knew he was in a rush to get to his 9 o'clock appointment. Tom the salesman. Tom the Real Estate Developer. Tom the builder. Tom the entrepreneur. He was good at what he did. And Joan had been right there with him from the very beginning. In the failing and the succeeding. She had always been his perfect helper. The perfect Proverbs 31 wife.

That morning there was hope filling her heart. Their marriage was stronger than ever. Despite all the difficulties. Despite the mistakes and heart-ache. When Tom looked at her that last time, he knew what he had in her. Her faithfulness was steady and sure. He left their home feeling like the lucky man that he was.

But, his time had come. They were waiting for him at the bottom of that long drive-way. Hiding out in the forever extending forest surrounding their home. Knowing the nearest neighbor was over a mile away.

Knowing no one would be looking. Knowing they wouldn't be caught. Joan later wondered if her husband somehow knew as he stood in that bathroom staring into the trees, feeling the eyes on him, knowing he was out of time.

But, that morning Joan never heard a thing. As she cleaned up breakfast and began loading the laundry to take to town for cleaning at the laundry mat, nothing seemed amiss. Until the phone rang. It was the office secretary wanting to know where Tommy was. It was after 9 o'clock and he had never showed. Mysteriously neither had the new customers who had scheduled the appointment.

'He must have gotten a flat,' thought Joan, which often happened on the miles of dirt road they had to drive to get to the office that was close to town.

Sadly, Joan was wrong about the flat tire. As she drove down the long, winding driveway in the Jeep Waggoneer packed with dirty laundry, her three-year-old son, her 5-month-old daughter, and her mentally-ill mom, Joan's heart stopped as she came to a halt behind

Tommy's old blue pick-up truck. Both doors wide open. Crutches in the back.

Slowly she opened her Jeep door and slid out silently. Silence. Nothing moved. Except Joan as she creeped toward something lying beside the truck.

Suddenly she froze. She knew. She saw the light blue sweater on the lifeless body. Her husband of nineteen years. Her adventurous Tommy. Gone.

All she could think was how final death was. The shock of it hit her hard as she mechanically slid back into her Jeep and expertly backed up the driveway, barely seeing the road through her tears. Her mother didn't say a word. The kids didn't make a whimper. They must have known, too. There was only silence as Joan made the call to the authorities who were not surprised.

Joan shouldn't have been surprised either. Tommy had been telling her this would happen. He had been forced to help the authorities catch the big fish they really wanted. Young Tom was small bait when they caught him and used him to get to that big catch. He never told Joan they had begged him to take his young family and hide in witness protection. But the authorities assured her when she questioned them that they did offer it to him in exchange for his cooperation, but he refused. He didn't think living in constant hiding was living at all.

The days after her husband's death left Joan's head spinning. She couldn't catch her breath, but somehow life had to go on. Her five young children needed her. She couldn't have stopped if she had wanted to. Revenge filled her mind. But life spun her along. Her heart laid bare. How could this happen? She was left with nothing but a pile of debts to be paid, children to feed and clothe, and a struggling business to run.

And here is where our heroine is truly born. The widow's might come to full fruition. My mom stood firm in the face of adversity. When others would run away in fear. She would stand firm. When others would lose faith. She would be faithful still. And when others would turn a blind eye. She would know God still cared.

And [Jesus] sat down opposite the treasury
and watched the people putting money
into the offering box.

Many rich people put in large sums.
And a poor widow came
and put in two small copper coins,
which make a penny.

And he called his disciples to him
and said to them,

"Truly, I say to you,
this poor widow has put in more
than all those who are contributing
to the offering box.

For they all contributed out of their abundance,
but she out of her poverty
has put in everything she had,
all she had to live on."
Mark 12:41-44

I always wanted to know more about this widow. I wondered at her story. Wondered about her. Marveled at her faithfulness. Then I realized, this widow is my mother. And I know her story well. Come and meet her. Joan. Our God-loving heroine. For she is truly a wonder to behold.

The Widow's Might: A Study Through Proverbs 31
also by CJP Navarro
Now Available on Amazon.com

www.ingramcontent.com/pod-product-compliance
Lightning Source LLC
LaVergne TN
LVHW041215080426
835508LV00011B/965